MW01483099

MIA
GETS IT

[signature] OCT 25

Avoiding Godot

Avoiding Godot

Anthology

Chris Chandler

9TH WAVE PUBLISHING

Oakland California, USA

Published by: Ninth Wave Publishing
Oakland, California, USA
www.ninthwavepublishing.com
info@ninthwavepublishing.com
USA (510) 842 0773

Ninth Wave Publishing LLC Second Edition

Title: Avoiding Godot - Anthology
Author: Chris Chandler ©2013

Book & Cover Design:
Jen Delyth & Chris Chandler
www.chrischandler.org

Cover Art: Jane Fisher ©2013
Back Photo: Susan Martin ©1990

Edited and typeset by:
Jen Delyth & Chris Chandler

Permissions Notes:
Most poems and collaborations have appeared in earlier publications as noted with each work.
Collaborations used by permission of author or authors.
Thanks to Philip Rockstroh www.philrockstroh.com

The artwork in this book consists mainly of collages created by Chris Chandler (for Blame or Credit.)
Many of the images contained in this book contain elements from sources found with a public
    domain heading.
The *Showtime Big Top Tent* is by Julie Leonardsson used by permission.
The 70s Dancers, *The Carnival Midway*, *The Sea Monkeys ad*, and the *Gas Mileage Wheel* are from
    free line art web sites. Public Domain.
The original image of *Eve and The Serpent* is from Coloring Kidz.
The *Food Not Bombs* Logo is by Keith McHenry and is used by permission.
The *IWW Poster* was designed by John Sloan and is used by permission of the IWW.

Ninth Wave Publishing
Second Edition ISBN 978-0-9833824-1-6
Published December 2013

www.ninthwavepublishing.com
www.chrischandler.org

Dedicated to

Claire C. Chandler

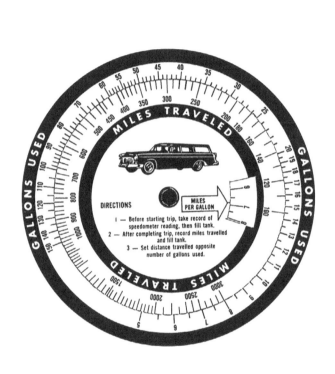

Contents

1. You Can't Comment on the Scenery Unless
   You Take the Trip

2. The World Was a Safer Place When Religion
   was the Opiate of the Masses Instead of
   the Amphetamine

3. She Holds Me in the Arms of the Sea

4. Reflections On Fun House Mirrors

5. The Split Second Between When the Trapeze Artist Flies and She Grasps the Hand of Her Catcher

6. Pay No Attention to That Corporation Behind The Flag

7. On the Set of A Cartoon Universe

8. "I AM NOT MAKING THIS UP!"

Foreward

For many years, Chris Chandler has been the best spoken word artist in America. Combining humor and outrage, wit, candor and a golden tongue, he has created a character as old as the hills and as new as the latest No Passing Zone sign. He has made the highways of America his stomping grounds and his mythology.

Like many a roving teller of tales, he has come into a town, regaled it, challenged it, transformed it — and then left it as mysteriously as he came upon it, onward to another room of hungry listeners, another crashed-on-couch, another meal of Slim Jims and gas station hot dogs, and stories upon stories upon stories.

The best way to experience Chandler, of course, is live and in color, in the room or in the crowd at the festival, watching the sweat and spittle fly, hearing the gasps and laughter and yelps of recognition from the assembled, like the acolytes of the Southern gospel preacher, which at bottom he is….

The next best is to hear the records, Chandler's inimitable rants woven through warm and ingenious threads of the best of American folk music.

These are not messages to comfort you in your repose, to soothe you while you sink further into couch-potatohood, but rather exhortations to act, to think, to question, yes — to rise up — against wrongness, unfairness, injustice, lack of feeling, lack of understanding.

Like Woody Guthrie, these are cries for the downtrodden, the marginalized, the undefended.

And if you are lucky enough to know Chandler's voice, that thousand-headed lariat of sarcasm and cornball, that singular southern siren, then you can hear his voice throughout these pages, whispering, chuckling, needling, blowering, raging.

These pages are not flat. They rise like cornbread. They are a written record, but they are a song. They are a pageant. You will want popcorn. You will want hot butter. You will want iced coffee. Just, please, not Starbucks….

You can read chronologically, but feel free to skip around. You may find what you need by chance. By happenstance. By damned good luck. There is life here, and experience, and enough knowingness to last any good road trip. Down to the store for some milk. Or to Burundi and back on a magical quest….

Come on in. Make yourself at home.
Anyone up for a story?

Dan Bern

Note from the Editor

It is my great pleasure to help put this anthology together. *Avoiding Godot*, represents a wide selection of work from the twenty five year career of someone I've admired as an artist, performer, poet, story-teller, for many years.

Chris Chandler on the stage, is an unforgettable experience. He is a force of nature, taking us on a journey that is both thought provoking and truly entertaining.

He is preacher and poet, rebel rouser and comedian, and an outstanding person to boot!

A Chandler performance always brings some tears with the laughter, whilst giving us both hard-hitting perspectives, along with tender reminiscence of our better selves.

Reading the words upon these pages, I can clearly hear his unique voice, feel the energy and undiluted passion that he brings to his live performance. A stylish, skinny bald man commands the stage – black trilby, suspenders, a well-pressed vintage suit. One road-worn leather shoe, balances effortlessly on the top of a well-travelled black metal chair, as he thrusts body and words up and out to us. Expressive fierce blue eyes, penetrate our hearts and minds, with humor and thought-provoking brilliance.

Many of you have experienced *The Chris Chandler Show*, have enjoyed the inspiring collage of music and song, poetry and storytelling, and often – if you are lucky – presented before a provocative projection of short films – a cartoon universe created by Chandler.

This book is a collection of spoken word, edited with an attempt to reflect some of the punctuation of the unique Chandler delivery, whilst giving the words readable space upon the page.

I respect this man as consummate artist, and love him as true friend.

Jen Delyth (May 2013)

Note from Chandler

I hit the road in May of 1988.

When I first started my Volkswagen and put Stone Mountain, Georgia in my rearview, Reagan was president. Gasoline was less than a dollar a gallon. The cold war was warm. The internet had seventeen users, and I was not one of them. Iran and Iraq were at war with each other. I had hair. I was writing material about Oliver North, Larry Flint and Jesse Helms.

Throughout this anthology, many of the references have dated, but the truth behind the rants remains the same. So I have included some material that may seem like ancient history. It is not. Americans think two hundred years is a long time. Europeans think two hundred miles is a long ways. It is not.

I know this, because there is not an interstate highway in the United States that I have not been on.

I have sung in truck-stop parking lots, trying to get gas money to make it to a demonstration or festival.

I have been through two Volkswagens, a Chevy LUV, a Datsun pick-up truck, a Dodge van, two Ford vans, a Ford pickup truck, an Oldsmobile, two Subaru station-wagons, and a Saturn station-wagon. Long may you run.

I have loved. I have been loved. I have lived.

Many characters fill these pages. They have colored my stories.
Without them my life would be a black and white coloring book,
waiting for you to pick up a crayon.
Thank you for coloring outside the lines!

In 1988 I had graduated from *The North Carolina School of the Arts*.
At college I was involved in a student group called *Onyx*, that produced original student plays. Although it was a highly competitive school where I was studying to be a stage lighting designer, I was equally competing with my own conflicting ambitions.

Onyx gave me my first taste of public performance. No matter how you carve it, it takes a while to put on a play, and I had begun writing skits and monologues faster than I could get them in front of an audience. So, I took to the streets and began performing them for unwitting passers-by in Winston-Salem, NC.

I noticed that people just walked by, thinking the guy on the street corner talking to himself must be crazy! What can I say? This was before the Bluetooth cell phones. (I think those people are crazy, but I digress.)

My way around this, was to borrow a friend's guitar. I didn't even know how to play guitar, but strumming it while I told monologues on the street corner, made me a folk singer. I started gathering small crowds. People actually put money in the guitar case. Can you believe it? I didn't.

When I graduated, I was going to cross the country, auditioning as a lighting designer at theatres. At that point I had not been beyond the states that bordered Georgia. In order to finance this summer wanderlust, I performed on street corners and subways.

I actually landed a job as an assistant lighting designer on Broadway, but was having so much fun as a street musician I turned it down.

I have not looked back. (Much to the chagrin of my parents, teachers and guidance counsellors...)

In the early days, I had a double cassette boom-box that plugged into my cigarette lighter, and as I rolled down the road I duplicated tapes, and sold them from my guitar case. The covers were copied on Xerox machines at pharmacies, that required one to put a dime in a slot in order to get a copy. There was no Kinkos. The cassettes had titles like *Stranded Musician Needs Gas Out of Town*, and *What? For This Price You Want Packaging Too?*

It was in Boston at Harvard Square, that this Georgia boy fell into his own. There I found a community of like-minded rebels and street performers. I joined a street musicians' commune. I was lucky enough to have stumbled into that scene, as a new folk explosion was detonating. I can think of dozens of folks that I either played the streets with, or jockeyed for position at open mics with, that are also celebrating a 25th anniversary about this time. Most are still making a living at it.

Being around those talented and knowledgeable folks was luck. Nothing premeditated about it, just dumb luck.

I am also fortunate to have been mentored by writers such as Phillip Rockstroh, well before my college days and beyond. He is a fine writer and I've included pieces that we collaborated on, especially from the first decade. I recommend you seek out his work.

In some cases, I have included passages from Rockstroh's brilliant stream of conscious mind, which have been trapped in the coffee filter of my voice - distilled into the right cup, to fit neatly in the plastic cup-holder hooked onto the window of my car. Such is the creative nature of the collaborative process.

Also, I was lucky enough to bump into Anne Feeney early on, at a time when I was considering giving up. She took me to my first demonstration, and inspired and encouraged me to keep writing. She remains my heroine. I was lucky enough to tour with her for about six years, and we made two records together. *We still call 'em records*! I recommend you check out her work.

Over the years I've teamed up with some of the best, creative, wonderful folks. It was back in Boston that Raelinda Woad suggested I set down the guitar and just do the monologues. Holy cow was she right! I am the worst guitarplayer who ever managed to make a living at it! I had landed a record deal with *Flying Fish Records* around 1992, and yes, that was a huge accomplishment, but no-one was buying a ticket to hear me play the guitar, and especially not sing.

Instead, I found people that could play and that could sing! And boy did I!

If nothing else, my bands have been as good as it gets. Amanda Stark, Dan Bern, David Rovics, Samantha Parton, Oliver Steck, Niki Leeman, Laura Freeman, Frankie Hernandez, Chad Austinson, Magda Hiller, Anne Feeney, Joanna Smith, and Paul Benoit to name a few. Thank you ALL!

I hope you enjoy these little tales, poems and collaborations set down on paper. They are divided loosely by themes, and in no chronological order. I've chosen them to represent the past few decades of work, and included some personal favorites.

Here's to the next twenty-five!

Chris Chandler
(May 2013)

if you were born in '33 you were 45 in '78

THANK YOU

To thank everyone that has helped me in my career would be impossible.

You know who you are.

Special thanks to Philip Rockstroh, for being my mentor in the early years, who was a creative collaborator and contributor to the material during the first half of my career.

Also Anne Feeney, for showing me the difference between being the devil and being a hell raiser.

And to all the musicians and song writers, who have brought these words to life on the stage. Most especially Anne Feeney, Paul Benoit, Frankie Hernandez, Magda Hiller and Amanda Stark.

Thank you to those that have helped with this anthology.

Most of all Jen Delyth, without whom this book would be a series of hand-written xeroxed pages stapled together.

And to Brian QTN for support and editorial skills.

I would also like to thank Dan Bern, Jane Fisher, Tom Noddy, and my extended and wonderful family for supporting me through the decades.

And most importantly "insert your name here".

– jcc

You Can't Comment on the
Scenery Unless You
Take the Trip

The United States
of Generica

I seen Jack Kerouac
in the back
parking lot of a Stop and Go.
He was pouring Wild Turkey
in a Slurpee
sittin' on the hood of a Yugo.

We went on the road on a changeless scene,
headlights rolled past my eyes
like the rolling flash of a Xerox machine.

Have we all gone blind,
from polystyrene signs,
endless replications,
of strip mall situations,
fast food attitudes,
and telemarketing platitudes?

What have they done to my road?
What have they done to my America?
The interstate made
The United States,
The United States of Generica.

I seen Walt Whitman, and Woody Guthrie
on the front seat of a '74 Camaro.
They were goin' down the road feelin' bad,
from bad burgers,
ordering food from a drive-through window.

With Holy Synchronicity,
and the luck of a tramp
we found ourselves
on the same off-ramp.

Would somebody
talk to me
about serendipity?

We ran
our Caravan
into the parking lot of a Piggly Wiggly,
where we all stared in awe
at a postage stamp of Elvis.
We all believed
that he was the king,
and agreed that poetry
has got no time for monarchy.

I heard a street corner poet say,
"Rock and Roll was once a threat,
but these days,
Rock And Roll is a Time-Life Anthology."

Rock and Roll will live for ever, Jack.
It lives on in the form of Muzak.
That's why I am shopping
for eternity.

Walt Whitman went wild
on the pharmaceutical aisle,
it was number twenty-one.
He did depart,
with a shopping cart
full of multi-colored condoms.

He said, "I sing the body electric,
but these days, I do it safely."

What have they done to my road?
What have they done to my America?
The interstate made
The United States,
The United States of Generica.

William Blake hitchhiking on Old Route 66,
I said, "Is it better out there in the sticks,
where there is not a sign of a K-Mart?
Did Ma and Pa sell the family store,
are they now employed
at the Walmart?"

He said, "Don't despair,
there is poetry everywhere."

We flipped up the electric windows
and clicked on the air
and told stories about hitchhiking quoting Baudelaire,
who said,
'If your gonna get drunk – stay drunk –
on wine, on virtue, on poetry."

William Blake once said,
"I had an epiphany looking in a single grain of sand."
We could all see eternity in a single grain...
...of Nutra-sweet.

But I am goin down the road feelin' bad.
I am goin down the road feelin' bad.
I am goin down the road feelin' bad,

But Woody Guthrie,
Like you taught me man,

I ain't gonna be treated this a-way.

By Chris Chandler and Philip Rockstroh
Originally released on the album *Generica* (1994) published in *Protection from all this Safety*
(1996) and on the album *Flying Poetry Circus* (2002)

Lightning Bugs and Barflies

Sometimes, on the road... when I'm tired... trying to stay awake...
I will listen to classic rock.

Because, it doesn't matter how old, how young, how middle aged you are...
you will go through the rest of your life listening to the music you listened to...
in the ninth grade.

And you will go the rest of your life dancing the way you danced... in the ninth
grade.

I was thinking about this while driving along the Pennsylvania Turnpike in mid
summer towards Pittsburgh, when I found myself driving through a sea of fire
flies.

The radio was playing *Stand By Me*, and the fire flies began to blink in unison
with the orange construction hazards.

I think back to the last time I was in Pittsburgh, back in March. I walked down
to my favorite little Irish bar to sit and write. Usually, this is a quiet Irish bar
where I drink Jameson and scribble silently until I have hallucinations of being
Dylan Thomas.

But on this, St. Patrick's Day weekend, my sweet little retreat has hired, of all
things a Karaoke DJ. A sign on the door announces that "Ladies Drink for Free."

The funny thing about fireflies is that it is only the male that flickers. They do
this in the hopes of attracting a female. If no female firefly can be found, males
will join forces and begin to blink in unison in hopes that their combined bril-
liance will reach the heart (or at least the thorax) of their beloved.

At the bar in Pittsburgh, barflies are garnished in blinking green shamrocks
and unbearable green paper hats, yet I cannot break from my own tradition.
After all, I came here to write, and this is what is happening.

I order a green beer, accept my own blinking shamrock, and find the only
open table.

Familiar acoustic guitar chords leak from the sound system as the Karaoke DJ rummages for a potential participant.

Stand... Stand By Me.

I wonder, what do fireflies think as they enliven their luminous bodies, captive in a giant mayonnaise jar. Do they dream of trying to pick themselves up by their tiny little bootstraps as they slide down the glass?

At the bar I get into an argument with a Libertarian who tells me, "The poor deserve what they get and they should pull themselves up by their bootstraps."

A single firefly escapes the windshield of my car and burns in a rhythm all his own. One lone brave soul steps to the karaoke microphone to intone the ubiquitous.

When the night has come
and the land is dark
And the moon is the only light we see.

Other lightning bugs announce their presence – one – then the other – and then – some unseen force makes two of them blink together – just once. Someone at the table next to me mutters beneath his breath:

No, I won't be afraid,
oh, I won't be afraid.
Just as long as you stand, stand by me.

Strangers saunter in and join in the chorus:

So darling, darling, stand by me.

Once-hollow eyes gleam like fireflies. Strangers clink glasses – and swear undying friendship – bound by lyrics inscribed upon our psyche by the tattoo needles of elevators, and grocery store ambiance.

At the bar, the Libertarian fumbles for change. I pick up his tab singing

Stand... Stand by me.

He continues his argument, citing Rosa Parks as an example of the individual at the heart of settling the world's tribulations.

I say, if you think a middle-aged seamstress from Montgomery, Alabama,
single-handedly started the civil rights movement,
then you probably think Lee Harvey Oswald, acted alone!

It occurs to me that the reason some people want us poor folks to pull ourselves up by our own bootstraps...

> ...is to get us to bend over.

The highway looks as if it were webbed by a single strand of Christmas lights – dazzling in harmony, blinking as one – while a thousand car radios are tuned to Rush Limbaugh spewing an alternate reality.

The whole bar sings together:

> *Darlin' Darlin' stand by me.*
> *Oh, stand by me. Stand by me. Stand by me.*

Aware of my own awkwardness in accepting the fact that such an absurd pop song has captured the zeitgeist of my generation, but too wrapped up in the group experience to care – I strike my cigarette lighter and hold it in the air.

Others follow suit. Cigarette lighters slice open the darkness.
The world is illuminated. I realize that we, like fireflies, are greater as a collective, as a whole – as a union – than we could ever be alone!

People begin to sway back and forth.
Strangers link arms. Some go home together.

Darkness descends, as one by one each solitary sparkle is extinguished.

But in that darkness...

> ...a new generation of fireflies...

> > ...is created.

Written in Pittsburgh in 2004
Originally released on the album
American Storyteller Vol 1 (2005) and *Matadors* (2012)

So Where Ya Headed?

So, where ya headed?

Of course… Dunno why I asked.

I mean you're standing on the side of the road with your thumb in the air holding a sign that clearly reads *Austin* and still, I have to ask.

Sometimes, I wish we all walked through this life holding a sign that announces where we are headed.

I guess now that I think about it, we do kinda carry one that announces where we've been – ya just gotta know how to read it.
But that's a different story.

Continue on Texas Farm Road 3721 for 437 miles.

Yea, it's a GPS. Whoda thunk that ten years ago?
A global positioning satellite pointed at my car, and I'd like it.
It's like a sign that announces where I am.

So, now that we know where we are, and where we're headed, I guess the only remaining question is:

Where ya coming from?

Oh yea? I like it out there. That's where they filmed *The Road Runner* cartoons.

Huh? The Music?

Oh, its satellite radio. I like it out here in the middle of nowhere. Though, I think its funny that they call it "Sirius." Named after the The Dog Star – Sirius. You know, the brightest star in the sky. At least it used to be.

Now the brightest star in the sky is (I am not making this up) the Nortel Satellite.

The very thing that the "Sirius" Satellite is named from has been given second class status by… well, The Sirius Satellite itself.

One of nature's greatest feats has been replaced by something man-made… like Barry Bonds beating Hank Aaron's home-run record.

Oh sure they named the company "Sirius" to "honor" its casualty.

To me, it kinda feels like naming your sports team "The Washington Redskins," or your subdivision "Nez-Perce Estates," or your town "Taos," or your state "Dakota" or your method of traveling across the high plains in search of buffalo wings a "Winnebago."

The only thing I know for sure is there aren't too many Delaware Indians living on Manhattan Island who can get the Shawmut Bank to give them a loan for a Cherokee.

Next to the Sun and the Moon, nothing in the sky has been written about more than that star. The Egyptians based their calendar on it. They used it to predict if it would be a hot dry summer or cold winter or if the Nile would reward her with her fertile flooding.

Me, I use it for the weather channel.

I like this channel here. The show's called "Disorder." They play the best of everything regardless of what genre it is – as long as it's good. Like you might hear Rachmaninoff played next to The Cramps, like yer supposed to.

'Cause if its good – it lasts. Like… like evolution. Like… say you're a bug, or a bird or a jelly fish, or an ape and you are good at being an ape or a jelly fish – odds are you're still here. There is no "order" to it.

You can't look at the stars and see a pattern like when you stare at the wallpaper in a Cracker Barrel. I mean, the stars are indeed wallpaper – but they are God's wallpaper, and God does not shop at Home Depot.

Although he does occasionally hire Mexicans out of the Home Depot parking lot just to piss off Republicans.

Well, yea – you're right about part of that… Texas is big… but I don't think it's ugly, In fact – I think it's beautiful! It has so far surpassed the zenith of ugliness – that it is flawless. It is perfect – even if it is perfectly ugly – and you can't argue that perfection in and of it self is not beautiful. It's just kind of an acquired taste – like gin and tonic, or the poetry of Rilke, or the later films of Mel Brooks. But I always say:

"You can't comment on the scenery unless take the trip."

It's like if you take a picture of any one place out in the middle of nowhere – it's ugly. Tumble weeds and dust. Cacti and cattle.   But when you drive across it… something cathartic starts to happen… It's hypnotizing… You see shit that's not really there… Or maybe, it was there all the time and you have to drive for 14 hours straight to find it?

When you drive from El Paso to Orange, you see the barren bluffs that go on forever, but then the moon rises, and some bug hits your windshield – just below the belt of Orion. And you look to Orion and you see the vastness of this landscape – The highway – our lives – as both vast and tiny.

It's like *Horton Hears a Who!* – only in reverse – and the elephant is running around the galaxy trying to get everyone in the universe to shout at once,

"We are here! We are here!"

So that we – here on earth – will know that heaven is out there.

The road does go on for ever.

Just like the stars,

and our lives,

and the poetry of Rilke,

and the music of Townes Van Zandt.

Written at the Kerrville Folk Festival in 2008
Originally released on the album *So, Where Ya Headed?* (2009)

9th Ward New Orleans, #2

9th Ward New Orleans,
the river has always run through you – but never so literally.

She has always been a part of you – but rarely like this.

Your nineteenth century widow's peaks are all that peek
from a river once held at bay by the hands of man.
Now, twenty-first century widows walk out on your widow's walks,
staring in vain for the horizon to materialize the lost.
But from the lost, your culture has always been found.

It is with you, 9th Ward New Orleans,
that the melting pot of America melts.

9th Ward New Orleans,
it is from you our culture has sailed in from all directions.

From wayfaring sailors seeking the roughest of trade
as well as barges filled with amber waves of grain.

Here the wholesome and the whore are changed forever. Wholesale.

Whether watching the tops of tankers crest the levees,
or endlessly rocking on stoops,
now on roofs,
watching the river flow on the streets below.

You are Alive!

9th Ward New Orleans.
As we watch your desperate desperadoes,
maybe now we know, they have always been there.
And that you, 9th Ward New Orleans
– like the lands beyond your levees –
have always been armed.
The desperate do desperate things when made more desperate.

But you, 9th Ward New Orleans,
have been made the lowest of the low.
But it is from the lowest of the low that our savior rises.

Like the savior born in the feeding trough of a jackass,
you really are the birth of the blues.

America does not understand that you cannot feel the joy of song
without the blue note of pain.
And it is pain you have felt.

So who can blame you when you never do ask
"Good Morning, America how are you?"

I don't recall America ever asking you.

9th Ward New Orleans,
Lake Pontchartrain once again had it's evil wicked way with you,
and you will bare this pregnancy for a coon's age.
A slow painful birth will come, as a distant trumpet joins your blues.

And when the world asks,
(and the world will ask...)
"What is that sound?"

A Caribbean accent will answer,
"It's just music. It's Jass Music – yes, it's Jazz music."

Your water will break.
And a new Louis Armstrong will spring from your loins
to blow his trumpet with the mouth of your river,
and that music, 9th Ward New Orleans,
will turn the gulf of Texaco back into the sea of Galilee.
Because, you 9th Ward New Orleans,

You are alive!

Written just outside New Orleans, late August 2005
Originally released on *American Storyteller Volume III* 2006

Oakland

(At the Corner of Poverty and Inspiration)

"That truck sounded like a woman singing," she said,
as the first sounds of Monday morning traffic made themselves
familiar with the Off Ramp Studio where I live.

It's like waking to the inspiration of a world in motion.

Oakland.

Oakland is the strained vocal chords of a croaky California
situated deep in the mouth of the San Francisco Bay.

At the Corner of Poverty and Inspiration.

Trucks and barges. Commuter trains and bicycles.
The BART whips by the third floor so close
you can pass notes to commuters.

Here at the corner of 880 and 580 there is a yellow truck stop,
and a blue collar bar that flanks the purple building as multi-colored
giant container ships unload truck-sized boxes upon
eighteen wheels of glass and steel.

Oakland.

The whole building vibrates with the sound of America
shouting through a mouth made of two interstate on-ramps,
that entangle and clover leaf 'round the building like
cords of Marigold feeding a ravenous America
with vessels full Chinese plastic, so she can defecate
discounted alien wares and with-alls out onto the green lawns
formed by the septic tank known as America.

Oakland.

Oakland has always been the Gateway to the East.
She was the start of the Intercontinental Railroad whose
golden spike was driven into the coffin of agrarian America in 1881.

Oakland.

The end of the line.
Weary easterners who followed the call "Go west, young man,"
could do so no more, unless they climbed aboard
ocean-bound freighters that filled her harbors. And many did.

It was the gold rush of '49 that brought so many to Oakland's shores, and
although there was little gold to be found, there was
plenty of timber with which San Francisco would be built.
But it was also the Gold Rush of '97 – the Klondike Gold Rush –
that fanned the flames of a nomadic nation
eager to migrate further into the vicious cold,
in search of a more viscous gold.

Oakland.

At the corner of Broadway and Embarcadero,
Jack London would embark upon such journeys
through that bitter cold, igniting infernos in many a restless heart.
His words are emblazoned,

"I would rather be ashes than dust."

But these days, it is dust – chalk dust – that outlines
the bodies of too many restless hearts
departing on a very different journey.

Oakland.

There is a plaque and a statue, and even a ritzy marina
named for the socialist and radical Jack London,
but there is no plaque or monument at the corner of 56th and Grove where
the socialist and radical Black Panther Party was formed,
offering free breakfasts to the children of a workforce that had served as the

anchor for Oakland's once humming wartime ship industry.
But when the shipping industry cut its chains and sailed,
it left its anchor to rust in the ghettos.

Oakland.

The Kaiser shipping industry recruited
hundreds of thousands of African-Americans
from primarily Louisiana in the '30s and '40s, creating
the blackest population in the United States west of New Orleans.
The smell of Cajun cuisine still mingles with jazz along cracked
sidewalks at the corner of Adversity and Revelation.

Oakland.

But all cities in America have their
duplicities, hypocrisies and underbellies.
Oakland is often viewed as the
poor, ugly step child of flowery San Francisco.

San Francisco is indeed a rose – and perhaps Oakland is the thorn.
But remember the thorn protects the rose
– without the thorn there could be no rose
– yet without the flower there is still the bush.

Oakland.

From Jack London to Bobby Seale and Huey Newton.
Sly and the Family Stone to Ed Kelly and Pharaoh Sanders.
Yoshi's to The AK Press, the Judi Bari bombing. Oscar Grant. Occupy.
The Black Giants and the Colored Elite to the Oakland Larks.
Bullet Meadows to Catfish Hunter and George Blanda.
The Black Hole. Black Panthers. Hell's Angels.

Oakland. Hella Oakland.

At the Corner of Poverty and Inspiration.

Written in a loft in Oakland, CA in spring 2010,
Originally released on the album *Matadors* 2012

Talkin' Bob Dylan and Woody Guthrie Blues

Out on the road, I often like to visit the hometown of my various idols.
Now, the time I'm thinking of I went to Okemah, Oklahoma.
That's right, I went to the hometown of Woody Guthrie.

Only once ya get there, what do you do? Ask the gas station attendant,
"Hey, would ya tell me about Woody?"

Well, that's exactly what I did. Only, everywhere I went, everyone I asked told
me the same thing,
"We don't know nothin' about no Communists around here, boy."

Well, y'all be proud a me... I refused to be defeated.

I wanted something to commemorate my visit.
Even if it was a T-shirt that read: "Okemah, Oklahoma 1st Baptist Church 2nd
Annual Bar-B-Q and Picnic", I wanted it.

I went to the hardware store. I went to the local cafe, I went to the drugstore.
In fact, it was in the drugstore when I saw it.
I was looking through the postcard rack.

They had the usual post cards such as the black one that reads,
"Oklahoma at night." They had "The Jackalope."
There, in the very back of the postcard rack, I spied it.

It was one of them old postcards, still had the old scalloped images on it.
On the back of the postcard it read, "US Postage ten cents."
On the front of the postcard it had a picture of Woody Guthrie's house,
and an old water-tower that read:

 "Welcome to Okemah, Home of Woody Guthrie."

I got real excited when I saw that and I ran up to the cashier and I said,

"Hey! I thought you said you didn't have nothing about Woody Guthrie – here's a picture of his house – where can I find it?

She said, "That old eyesore? They tore it down about ten years ago."

I said, "Well what about this water-tower?"

"Oh, it's still there – ya go down the main road about a mile or so and you'll see it."

So I went down the main road about a mile or so and I did indeed see it. Only, It no longer said, "Home of Woody Guthrie" on it.

Well, y'all be proud of me. I refused to be defeated.

I wanted to get up close to the water tower – maybe I could see through the peeling paint where it used to say "Home of Woody Guthrie" on it.

So, I got off the main road and on to this little dirt road that pulled me up behind the water tower and that's when I saw it. I am not making this up!

Facing the forest, not facing the highway – for all the squirrels to see – it did indeed say, "Home of Woody Guthrie."

I figure, "That side was made for you and me!"

I said, "Hey Hey The interstate!"
Ridin' down the road now I feel great.
They got gas station hotdogs,
they are two for ninety-nine.
And down in Louisiana,
there's some really cheap wine.

Well, on my way out of town, I picked up this hitchhiker.
Kind of an unsavory lookin' fellow.
He had lots of tattoos and piercings in places we won't talk about.

I only know that, because he showed me.
I didn't ask him to show me, he just did.

About the time he was showing me I looked in the rearview and saw the red and blue lights of the Oklahoma State Troopers. The Cop came up to the window,

"Boy, I clocked you at fiddy-sebum in a fiddy-five. Not only that, your right rear tail-light's out, and that uhhh passenger you got there wid ya... he ain't got his safety belt on. I believe you are in a little trouble there, boy. You wanna step from the vehicle?"

Now, he put me in the back of the cop car, and if you've ever spent any time in the back of the cop car you know you are actually in trouble.

He had the usual questions,
"What are you doin' here in Oklahoma from Georgia, Boy?"

"Just passin' through, Sir. I wasn't plannin' on stoppin' unless I needed some of that fine Oklahoma gasoline. Best gasoline in the country now, yes Sir!"

"What do you do for a living'?"

"Ummm... I'm a musician."

"What kind of music do you play, boy?"

Well, incase you haven't figured out by now, I have a hard time answering that question. I figured I'd just skip it and I said, "Folk music."

"Folk music? You mean like Woody Guthrie?"

I figured, what the hell, "Yes Sir, like Woody Guthrie."

There was a long pause, and he said,
"Well don't tell nobody but I love Woody Guthrie, I'm gonna just give you a warning!"

I said, "Hey Hey the interstate!"
Ridin' down the road now I feel great.
They got gas station hotdogs,
they are two for ninety-nine.
And down in Louisiana,
there's some really cheap wine.

Well, about a year passed, and I found myself in the home of another idol. I found myself in the home town of Bob Dylan,
Robert Zimmerman from Hibbing, Minnesota.

Now, my experience in Hibbing was a little different.

First thing I saw was this giant neon sign, piercing the darkness, that read, "Zimmy's."

I got real excited and grabbed the first parking spot I could find.
And I ran in there expecting to see some old folk singers still singing *The North Country Blues.*

But instead was a bunch of middle aged, middle class people singing
(and I am not making this up.) *The Flying Purple People Eater.*
Yes, The bar named after the poet of a generation was indeed... a karaoke bar.

But they did have Bob Dylan's high school yearbook picture right there on the menu. I sat down at the bar and ordered up the Zimmy Burger and thought,

"I'm going back to New York City, I do believe I've had enough."

Now, on my way out of town, I picked up a hitchhiker.
Then I got pulled over. This time for doin' forty-two in a forty-five. Cop said, "Anyone going that slow must be drunk."

He had me get in the front of the cop car this time and he had the usual questions.

"What are you doing in Minnesota from Georgia, Boy?"

"Just passin' through Sir, wasn't planning on stopping unless I had to purchase some of that fine Minnesota gasoline. Best Gasoline in the country, Yes Sir."

"What do you do for a living'?"

"Ummm, I'm a musician."

What kind of music do you play?"

I was thinking, "Wait a second, I've seen this movie."
I figured I'd just skip it and said, "Folk Music."

"Folk music, ya mean like Bob Dylan?"

I figured, "What the hell..." and said, "Yes sir, like Bob Dylan."

"You're the third one this month. Last one had four ounces of marijuana on him, you wanna get in the back of the car while we search your vehicle?"

I just put my feet up on the grate between the seats knowing full well they weren't going to find anything, except maybe some bootleg Bob Dylan tapes.

I said, "Hey Hey The interstate!"
Ridin' down the road now I feel great.
They got gas station hotdogs,
they are two for ninety-nine.
And down in Louisiana,
there's some really cheap wine.

Written in Hibbing, MN 1989
Originally released on *American Storyteller Vol II* 2006

The World Was a Safer Place
When Religion was the
Opiate of the Masses
Instead of the Amphetamine

Matter

I looked past the curvature of the earth, into the heavens,
past the myriad of stars and galaxies and planets all
swirling expanding and contracting
– just beyond the dust on my windshield
– and I shouted up to
God himself,

"I MATTER!"

And God responded, "Why, yes. Yes, you are."

At that point I realized I really am one with God.
Only once you become one with God,
do you then have to pray to yourself?

I hope not, because I'm the kind of rebel that thinks that on those rare
occasions whenever I am in charge – I feel a need to question my own
authority. I find myself looking in the mirror shouting

"Don't let ME tell me what to do!"

Personally, I always thought that what the bible meant when it said
we were created in God's image – is that he created us while looking in the
mirror and therefore did it all backwards... (explains a lot).

That's what I don't get. God made us in his image,
yet he made each and everyone of us different. (Well, except for me.)
So, that must mean God is... well... different.

Just like every snowflake, and every speck of dust on my windshield.
Just like the planets, the heavens, the stars, our lives.
It's all one big Merry Go Round...
The days, the years, the seasons, they go round.
We wave to our parents as we pass...
they wave back... and then... they are gone.

We see people on their high horse, a brass ring just out of reach.
They reach, but down they go down again.
The band has been replaced by a calliope that makes
Entrance of the Gladiators sound like *Pop Goes the Weasel.*
No-one seems to mind – and in the end we wind up
right back where we started.

Sometimes we dream.
Sometimes we dream big.
Which is why I rolled over this morning and mashed the snooze
button saying, "I must keep the dream alive!"

In the dream, I was standing on the side of the road.
There was traffic, lots of traffic.
On the other side of the road there was this chicken taunting me saying,
"Who are you to question my motives?"

I started to cross the street, and then changed my mind wondering if
I was as indecisive as I used to be. I shouted back,
"Just because I changed my mind doesn't mean I'm not still right!"

The reason I did not cross the road, was I wanted to go down it.
"Going down the road feeling bad,"
with a rubber chicken hanging from my rearview.

I don't know about you, but I would rather hang with someone
who is looking for answers, than someone who has found them.
Whether or not I have ever found any answers I do not remember.
Having a bad memory is the only thing that gives me a clear conscience.

Sometimes my conscience bothers me – but my conscience is
just another one of those voices in my head – like God.
Just because I'm pretty sure the voices in my head aren't real
doesn't mean I shouldn't listen to them.
I mean,
I listen to the news and I am pretty sure that isn't real.

The voices in our head may be all we have.
Sure, God created the stars, but who created the constellations?

Who sat beneath the stars and told a story,
as someone else listened, painting pictures in the sky?
Those images stayed in his head till he carried them to a cave
and painted them on the walls.
Someone else saw the picture – and told another story.
Every picture tells a thousand stories
and every story paints a thousand pictures.

You do the math. Count the stars.

When you do, the math distills the story down to another picture – which is
totally abstract – and the universe becomes
a giant Jackson Pollock.

God is up there randomly spilling paint.
Deliberately throwing paint.
Carefully placing tight detailed lines... drawing an arrow to a thought...
and the thought is boiled down to a haiku.
which is:

Haikus are obscure
Often hard to understand
Refrigerator

The truth is:
The power of good is greater than the power of evil
– just not by very much.

It is a struggle... the future is... but it can be predicted.

Because what is ahead of us, depends
solely upon what is inside us.

Written in Oakland, CA (2012)
Previously unreleased

The Silverware of Heaven
Ain't Safe Around Me

Scientists say they have found traces of vinegar drifting in space, and they say vinegar is the building block of life.

Vinegar, the stuff wine turns into, when you don't screw the cap on just right.

The way I figure it is them starry heavens must be full to bursting... with wine. But by the time it gets to us... vinegar.

And here I am on Earth lookin' up and it's no wonder I have a bitter taste in my mouth.

Them stars glint at me like champagne glasses,
and all I can do is look up at 'em like you look
when your rich fancy neighbors is havin' a party
and it's clear you ain't invited.

Well, all right then, I guess they ain't gonna invite us to their party.
But the question is: what are we down here on Earth gonna do about it?

Do we storm Heaven and crash the thing?

I reckon we'd be terribly out of place.

Stumbling about amongst the sequined outfits of diamond stars
– us in our street clothes – stickin' out like a plate of armadillo roadkill
on a banquet table of fresh fruit, imported cheese and that paté.

Do I act like them workin' man's heroes The Three Stooges – stealing cheese-balls from the banquet table and slipping them in to my tattered overalls?

No. The silverware of heaven ain't safe around me.

Or should I just do what they tell me on gospel TV
and admit my wretchedness!

Telling all my betters that if they're ever feelin' in a down-scale mood then come on down here and go slummin' at the trailer court we call Earth.

Yea, the whole thing is a trailer court!

I mean think about what they see from Heaven when they look down on us. All the space junk orbiting our front yard: space lab, rocket parts, satellites sitting up on blocks – while we suck down malt liquor,
and smoke generic cigarettes, and gossip bitterly 'bout our dumb-shit inbred relations in our underprivileged, incestuous world.

Oh Momma Earth, why didn't you teach us no better?

You was always wearin' that tacky revealing tube-top made of clouds, while pining away for Daddy.

(Who, they say, conceived us when he came down here slummin', drunk on a DNA cocktail of primordial ooze...
He left the next eon and we ain't seen him since.)

Me, I just want to tear ass through the heavens in a souped-up muscle car spaceship – a Barracuda UFO gone Super Chevy Nova.
I say, to hell with all them snotty angels. And I'll be yellin',

"If you think you're better than me how come your chariot ain't got no duel exhaust, glass pack or a hood scoop!
So if you snobby bastards won't love me as I am,
then at least you'll know I was here!"

HELL YEA!

We're backwards and crude down here on Trailer Court Earth
 – but at least I got me a double wide...
and you bet your celestial ass...
we're full of piss
and vinegar!

But goddamn, if that blacktop of a night time skyway ain't beautiful!

'specially if you got some honky-tonk angel beside you
in the bucket seat of your UFO GTO.
The laws of class gravity have been defied
just by the rebellious act of daring to feel one hundred percent alive!

So don't weep too much for me Momma Earth.

Our trashy lives might be short, meaningless, and ignorant down here,
but at least them snobby stars can look down here every now and again, and
while they're actin' like they're bein' sick to their hoity-toity stomachs over the
way we carry on, they might just wonder,
"Who the hell was more alive – us or them?"

'Cause they know, I was.

Right before I missed that sharp curve in the wormhole
and crashed into an oncoming comet and flamed out
like an explosion in a South Carolina fireworks factory.

So don't weep for me none, Momma Earth.

By Chris Chandler and Philip Rockstroh
Originally published in *Protection From All This Safety* (1996)
and on the album *Hell Toupee* (1999)

God Fearing Agnostic

At the airport, they asked me, "Mr. Chandler, what is your final destination?"

I answered, "Well, Heaven I hope."

And I do. Really. I am no atheist, my friend.

I am a God-fearing Agnostic.

Though, I do think the world was a safer place when religion was the opiate of the masses instead of the amphetamine.

But don't worry, I'm not going to get all fundamentalist on you. I don't like fundamentalists of any kind – including atheists.

Them fundamentalist atheists, they don't wanna capitalize the word God. I'm like, "Why not? Ya capitalize *Huckleberry Finn* don't ya?"

And then they wanna take "One Nation under God" out of the pledge of allegiance. I don't have a problem with the phrase, " One Nation under God."

What I have a problem with is…
                                            …people pledging allegiance.

What does "One Nation under God" mean anyway?

What does that make Australia?
Are they more under God than we are?
Is Canada "One Nation on top of God?"
Or is God all around us?
Perhaps we should be, "One Nation in the center of God?"

Personally, I think we should be. "One Nation getting over God."

And scientists – they don't know.

They are always trying to switch some facts to fit some theory.
They have been since Eve pulled the apple off the tree of knowledge and dropped it on Isaac Newton's head.

But why an apple?

I mean the Bible never says.

What if it were a banana?
I bet a whole lot more people would read the Bible
if it had a snake talking to a naked chick getting her to inhale a *Chiquita*.

And then he punishes the snake by making him crawl on his belly for the remainder of his days? I mean...
                                    ...he's already a snake.

It is ironic that the evil serpent is responsible for getting Eve
to put her clothes ON!

> *My friend Brino always says,*
> *I can count all the seeds in an apple,*
> *but who can count all the apples in a seed?*

So what if it were a banana she ate?

There would have been no Johnny Appleseed.
There would have been a Johnny Bananaseed.
Only, these days, bananas don't have seeds.
So, the guy would have gone around the country grafting banana stalks.

William Tell would have shot a banana off his son's head.

I would be using a *Banana iPhone*.

The Beatles would have released their records on *Del Monte*.

Sir Isaac Newton would not have had his 'eureka moment' when an apple hit him in the head, he would have slipped on a banana peel.

One day he's just walkin' along and his foot hits
a banana peel lying on the sidewalk.
His foot goes up in the air, and he comes down
– KA-BAM! – like an anvil in the *Road Runner* cartoon,
which is where he comes up with the concept of gravity.

The stars are circling around his head...
and then he's staggering around all dazed and lookin' all Courtney Love – lyin'
there on the ground lookin' up.

('Cause we all know that both astronomers and musicians spend a lot of time
on their backs)

And he's lookin' at all them stars and them constellations...
He sees Andromeda... Aquarius... Buster Keaton...

But so many stars are spinning around his head
that he concludes he is the center of the universe – and ya know what?

He's right.

Not 'cause he's Sir Isaac Newton,
but because the universe is infinite.
From wherever you stand it is equal distance in any direction,
and that by definition IS the center.

So because Eve eats a banana instead of an apple,
we don't get no big bang theory,
we get the "God Slipped on a Big Banana Peel Theory."

If that were the case, hell, I'd believe in intelligent design.

But the way I understand it,
intelligent design
is the most self-centered concept
human beings have ever come up with.

I mean I don't know about you, but I wouldn't want to
belong to a universe that would have me as its center.

I am the guy who said,
"People who believe life is great simply have nothing to compare it to."

I say, "Life is short cruel and unfair."

But the good news is… it is equally unfair to everybody.

So, the next time you are sitting there saying life is particularly unfair to you –
get over it – 'cause quite frankly, you are just not that special!

Written in Silver Spring, MD in 2008
Originally released on the album *So, Where Ya Headed?* (2009)

Sofas and Practical #2 Pencils

At times I feel enmeshed
in the loneliness and longing of all things,
asking myself, "What would I rather be?"

I wonder if inanimate objects ask the same questions.

Sometimes I'm convinced that an exhausted sofa will sigh,
longing to be a hammock tethered between two palm trees,
swaying in a tropical breeze.

The hammock sighs
longing to be a magnificent bed in a luxury hotel,
where two champagne-sipping sophisticates
meet for an illicit tryst.

The cigarette lighter they use after their stolen hour,
sighs in a crazed desire to be the eternal flame,
that illuminates a graveyard of forgotten soldiers,
who gave their life in a forgotten war.

The forgotten war sighs
"I wish I were just a quiet evening at home."

I hear the loneliness and longing of all things.

I wonder, do the practical #2 pencils of accountants
fantasize about drawing bawdy pictures
of urban sophisticates in a luxury hotel?

Does the luxury hotel dream
of dropping its facade of rectitude,
and becoming a flop-house?

Quartering a poet, sprawled on an exhausted sofa,
composing brilliant, unpublishable verse,
while being pestered by bill collectors on telephones

which grow disgusted of tormenting
the multitudes for niggling sums
so that those telephones begin orating
The Sermon on the Mount?

Does *The Sermon on the Mount* fantasize
about becoming a Vegas lounge act?

What if there was a great awakening of atoms.
Where they all remembered their
vast and intricate histories.
An Atomic explosion of memory.

We might hear the tale
of a fleck of lint floating in the air,
that had once been a part of a soldiers bootlace,
that he gave to his beloved to lace her corset,
the night before he died...
...in a forgotten battle
...in a forgotten war.

A fleck of lint,
that was once part of the molecular structure
of a Bushman's pelt,
which contained the tooth of a sabertooth tiger,
which evolved into an alley cat,
that was gutted, to make the strings of a violin,
which entertained elegant guests
in a luxury hotel.

That fleck of lint now has nothing
but time on it's hands.
To float in the air,
and sing of love,
of war,
of mythical beasts,
of beauty, of poverty, of sadness,
of joy.

That fleck of lint
now drifts unnoticed into your beer.

You drink it down...
and it sees
the joys and sorrows of your life,

until you are buried, forgotten in the earth.

But you will rise again as grass,
which is eaten by cows,
who go to slaughter,
and are served
in a luxury hotel...

and washed down with a beer,
we all get to see

Saturday night...
...all
...over
...again.

By Chris Chandler and Philip Rockstroh
Originally published in *Protection from All This Safety* (1996)
and on the albums *Convenience Store Troubadours* (1997and *Collaborations* (1998)

G Chord

What does a fly see when it lights on a mirror?
Does it register vanity?

Does it pause and comb its antennae
or contemplate the slight overbite to its mandible?

What does a fly hear
when it flies through a room where Mozart is playing?

What divine music surrounds us every moment
of every hour of every day that we do not hear?

Does that mean the music is not there?

It occurs to me that everything is made of molecules,
reverberating, forever undulating, like
Jacqués Brel, Ma Rainey, Johnny Cash, and Duke Ellington.

All matter is in constant motion.
Only, some vibrates so fast that it seems to us to be solid.
Which for us, being solid objects ourselves, is rather convenient.
Otherwise, we would pass through each other,
like low bass tones pass through thin walls,
and cops from other dimensions would come tell us
to turn our stereos down.

Still there are some out there that say,
"Give me the familiar, let me hear
Hotel California just one more time.
Give me hard, unflinching, empirical facts.
I need sheet music for jazz. Seduce me with realism.
Don't get me drunk on cheap poetry,
then try take advantage of me."

They don't realize that it is
within that moment of infinite uncertainty

that we are able to
hear the note
that comprises the chord
that generates the phrase
that builds the stanza
that defines the work
that is the world in which we walk...

Our lives hang in the air like musical notes.
Sometimes we lift towards heaven
like the angels of Chagall,
or we slip downward to the
terrestrial baritone of a Leadbelly ballad.

Either way, all is Coltrane.

Louie Armstrong still sings Cole Porter, and we are
walking on, standing on, sleeping
on music.

Open a window! Eavesdrop on God!
Turn off your radio and hear it.

Everything is made of molecules,
vibrating like the strings of a guitar, like the head of a drum,
like the frequency of my voice.
In fact we are standing upon a giant G chord.

Perfect pitch must be attained by the imperfect musicians,
within this world of infinite uncertainty,
in order to create a world,
where all is song...
...all is song...
...all is song.

By Chris Chandler and Philip Rockstroh
Originally published in *Protection from All This Safety* (1996)
and on the albums *Collaborations* (1998) and *Hell Toupee(1999)*

Evil (is boring)

Come gather 'round me people.

I would like to talk to you about something that we all have in common.
Yes, my friends I would like to talk to you about...

EVIL.

Now let's get one thing straight here from the very start –
that evil is not what you are thinking.

Evil is boring!

Evil does not cause prepubescent girls' heads to spin around
and levitate household furniture and appliances.
Evil causes you to want to own those household appliances
in the first place!

Evil is when you're at a party,
and you're eyein' some beautiful some someone,
and some beautiful some someone is eyeing you.

So, you make your way over to that beautiful some some someone,
when some schmuck comes up to you
and starts talking to you about automobile insurance
– and you find yourself interested in that conversation.

You, my friend, have embraced... Evil.

Evil does not come flying out of hell
wearing leathery wings, bearing some Faustian bargain.
Evil comes in the form of some insipid game show host.
Evil is behind door number one.

Evil does not have claws or talons.
Evil wears press-on nails.

Evil does not have cloven feet or a hairy satyr back.
Evil is the hair club for men.

(And remember my friends,
I am not just the president,
I am the very embodiment, of Evil.)

Compulsive complacency.
Excited by insipidity.
Possessed by banality.
The demons of normality.

Plagued by the pedestrian.
I've been to hell and back again.
I'm wearing the devil's cardigan.
I'm wearing the devil's cardigan.

Evil does not cause adolescents
to form rock 'n roll death cults
while they're in their acne-prone years.

Evil comes in the form of the PTA to impose dress codes.
After all, what could be more evil
than to tell a teenager
to dress like he is middle-aged?

Evil does not speak to you through a Ouji board.
Evil speaks to you through trivial pursuit.
Evil is boring
– and board games are called that for a reason.

The devil wants you to be bored.
The devil wants you to be boring.

The devil wants you to sit at home
–frozen in a Stygian Lazyboy –
channel-surfing through the 59 circles of hell!

Floating in remote control limbo,
slouching ever-towards 1-900 numbers,
infomercials, *The National Anthem*,

until your whole body turns to
nothing...
but ...
static!

But there is hope!

Because, if the devil is the Lord of the Bored...
then there shall be redemption in

– the ridiculous!

So, if you are the kind of person
that would read a book like this,
(as if it were poetry)

then you shall be canonized...

as a saint.

By Chris Chandler and Philip Rockstroh
Originally released on the album *Generica* (1994)
and published in *Protection from All this Safety* (1996)

Would You Die For a Necktie?
(thoughts on fabric #2)

I was riding along. Listening to the radio.

When I look out the window and see this box of used clothing –
80's style – polo shirts, men's suits with padded shoulders and gothic lines,
Reagan-era beauties cast out to the sidewalk
looking stunned at the new era.

I began having a crisis of my own mortality, and I thought...

After we die – do our souls laugh
about our cast off bodies
the way we might snicker over a dated necktie?

Will our most passionate beliefs
seem nothing more than a big pair of silly shoes
that we loved in our youth?

More and more my convictions seem to dangle from me
like a wide necktie – 70s style – tied in a Windsor knot,
thick as a cowbell beneath my chin.

Some people have convictions for which they will kill.

They'll claim that the cloth of their convictions
was cut from the omnipotent tailor above.
Some as serious as the buckles on the shoes of a 17th century puritan...
Some as oppressive as a 21st century Burqa...
Some as ridiculous as the intergalactic-A-GoGo gear
of *Star Trek* aliens (original series.)

Would you die for a necktie?

Would you kill for views
that in the future will look as ridiculous as platform shoes?

Ancient people believed
that fate was basically a fashion designer,
spinning the yarns of destiny on a loom of time.
All was preordained by some cruel cosmic Calvin Klein.

Today, fallen angels of fabric that we are,
we ignore the fashion tips of the gods
and outfit ourselves in convictions of our own design.

The Haute Couture of Freewill.

Still, somehow it is our free will that leaves us standing
in cheap man-made materials – sewn in some exploitive country
– distant within ourselves.

We sit mournful and numb before a whirl of sewing machines.
Underpaid. Confused by our condition.
Dreaming. Forever dreaming...
of the black silky oblivion of sex
– the unknown fabric of life and death.

Ninety percent of the universe is made of an unknown fabric
– dark matter.
The same percentage exists in our minds.
Ninety percent of the dark matter in our brains we do not use.
But this means there is endless potential for new design.

First you must not mind the endless cutting and tearing of fabric.
Endlessly submitting yourself to the
crucifixion nails of needle and bobbin.

Oh angels of fabric!
Release me from this scorching polyester wasteland
where I currently exist...
For I have seen the holy tablets...
                    ... and I'm on God's worst dressed list.

By Chris Chandler and Philip Rockstroh
Originally published in *Protection from All This Safety* (1996)
and on the albums *Collaborations* (1998) and *So, Where Ya Headed* (2009)

Blood to Wine

Christ said, "My blood is the wine."

This might lead one to the conclusion, that
the Antichrist's blood is...
non-alcoholic.

In fact I think that proves it:
the Antichrist is indeed responsible
for non-alcoholic beer.

I mean it's expensive,
tastes like Sh...
...Schaefer...
...Light.

You wake up the next morning,
with all the regret, had none of the fun,
and you had to drive.

Yes, Christ said, "My blood is the wine."
He also said,
"I am the light. I am the way. I am a fisher of men."

Can't you see him out there on that boat with the disciples?
Don't you think this sounds like a recipe for a
tragic alcohol-related boating accident?

Some say this is the way to salvation.
I think it sounds more like happy hour.

I mean, he fed the multitudes with two fish and a loaf of bread.
He turned the water into wine…
Jeez, no wonder he's got so many followers these days.
Hell, I'll listen to anybody as long as they're
buying the drinks and it comes with an open buffet.

Now myself, I have been a frequent worshipper
at The Holy Cathedral of the Eternal Last Call.

One evening, on the way home,
I was pulled over at a DUI roadblock for having
too much love of the Lord in my veins.

I reminded the cop,
"Christ said, 'My blood is the wine,'
and I only had the two drink minimum."

The cop said,
"Oh you've been hanging' out with that guy.
Last time we pulled him over,
you should have seen his blood-alcohol content.
We pulled him out of the car and sure enough,
he walked on water
– but not in a straight line."

I don't know, but I'd like to find
That in Heaven you can drink wine all the time.
But I'm so broke, have pity on me,
I can't buy a drink down in New Orleans.
So Mercy Me, Oh Mercy My,
I wanna go to Heaven Lord, 'fore I die.

Personally, I've always thought
they should have DUI - type roadblocks
where they arrest really dull people.

"I'm sorry sir, you'll have to come with us,
obviously you're going to bore people."

Not only that, but they should have holding tanks
where they keep them through the weekend.
Oh, in fact I think they already do: it's called Starbucks.

I can just hear hardened criminals, right now saying,
"Put me in the cell with the rapists, the murderers,

but don't send me to Starbucks."

I don't know, but I'd like to find
That in Heaven you can drink wine all the time.
But I'm so broke, have pity on me,
I can't buy a drink down in New Orleans.
So Mercy Me, Oh Mercy My,
I wanna go to Heaven Lord, 'fore I die.
Wouldn't ya know – it's just my luck,
Heaven's been bought out by Starbucks.

Christ said,
"My blood is the wine...
not a double iced frappuccino."

Perhaps in Revelations
there was some veiled, cryptic reference
to a double iced Frappuccino.
I've often suspected that the writers of that book
were feeling a bit jittery and under extreme sleep depravation.
Perhaps this is why the beast slouches towards Bethlehem...
Slouching because he's a bit grumpy and groggy:
he hadn't had his morning coffee.

Perhaps, the prophets foresaw
a Starbucks opening in the Holy Land,
– that's how they knew the final days would be upon us.
Maybe that's why God didn't take the call,
when Christ called to him from the cross.
He hadn't had his morning coffee.
There was no Starbucks. Yet.

Can you imagine what the conversation
would have been like if he had taken the call?

"Father, why hast thou forsaken me?"

And God gets the call... overworked, tired,

perhaps contemplating a long overdue vacation,
maybe even trying to switch to decaf:

"All right! All right!
Put him through but make it brief.
I got a typhoon scheduled for mid-afternoon in the South Pacific.

"I also have a situation in the Mediterranean
– some dumb kid wearing a pair of Cretan-rigged wings
– held together with wax or something
– flew too close to the sun and crashed into the sea.
There could be litigation.
Folks are saying that I should put up a warning label across the sun.

"In the Yucatan some crazy Mexican king
just tossed about ten thousand people into a volcano,
as some kind of a tribute to me...

"...It was a nice gesture of course.
I was touched – flowers would have been nice too.

"So, as you can see I have my hands full...
I guess now that I think about it, you do too...
hanging there on the cross and all...

"Tell ya what, call me back on Sunday,
my slow day, I'll pencil you in for a resurrection...

"...then after that let's take a little time off,
a long millennium, or two.
I've been looking at some pleasant
retirement property in the Pleiades.

"You try and support an entire universe,
and see if YOU are much fun at parties...

"...It's not like I can get away for a wild weekend,
like that drunk brother of yours.
You think you've got problems...

What am I going to do about Dionysus?
He's gone and joined a twelve step program.
Starts talking to me about relinquishing control.
Somebody's got to be in control around here.
I'm God. I have to be a control freak.

It comes with the territory.
He starts telling me to give myself over to a higher power
– how in the blazing blue heavens can God
give himself over to a higher power?

"Oh, and another thing...
What's with these existential philosophers
who keep saying I'm dead.
I didn't die, I quit!

"Now if we can just get man to shut up too.
I can't get any sleep with all this yak yak yak.
They won't shut up.
Sure I'm supposed to hear every sound
– every sparrow falling.

Sure, I used to hear it.
It used to wake me up out of a deep sleep
– but these days – I can't sleep.
Who could?
Knowing the future is coming and it's your fault.
There will be all these people down at some place called Starbucks
going yak yak yak – It makes me long for falling sparrows.

"I sent you down there with a pretty basic message:

Quit your job,
drink some wine,
be nice to each other.

The next thing I know, they are nailing you on a cross,
then everybody's wearing some model of that cross around their neck.
Nobody wants to take a drink – and nobody wants to take the day off.

"If I can't get them to listen to that
how can I get them to listen to anything?
But I'll say it again:

The wine is my blood.
Relax. Take it easy.
Have a glass or two...

"If you don't want to be a fundamentalist about it
– an umbrella drink is nice also.

But whatever you do,
don't try the non-alcoholic beer."

By Chris Chandler and Philip Rockstroh
Originally published in *Protection from all this Safety* (1996)
and on the album *Convenience Store Troubadours* (1997)

Afterlife

There is a light
that wakes us up,
and gets us out of bed each day.

It is not the blue neon of digital clocks
announcing a central point
in a specific time zone.

Nor the orange ball breaking the horizon,
creating the very time zones of day and night.
Though it does create its own time zones...

Here.

Now.

Back then,

and tomorrow.

The light of life creates and crosses
each of those horizons.

There are those that believe
in an afterlife.

I am one of those.

But afterlife is as complex
as the soap operas of our daily lives.

As simple as human history itself,
as misunderstood as the pearly gates,
as over interpreted as the River Styx.

After life is simply that:

After...

Life...

It is the life we leave here on Earth.
The world we have helped create.

They have left for us
a perfect Heaven,
through the light they have shown.

That is the light
that gets us out of bed each day...

May we continue to shine their light

right here,

in the Heaven that they have created.

So that others may feel it,

right here,

in the After Life.

Forever.

Originally released on the album
American Storyteller Vol II (2006) and *Matadors* (2011)

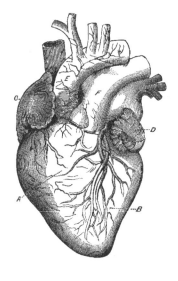

She Holds Me
In the Arms of the Sea

9th Ward New Orleans #4

I am in love with a drunk.

Oh sure she functions, like most alcoholics do.
But, isn't every drunk, at least on some level,
a functional alcoholic?

One man's dysfunctional is another man's high achiever.

Depends on your expectations, I suppose...
but I don't think she has ever many of those.

It is both her beauty and her blemish.

She is easy.
She is Big Easy.

She has one of those jobs
where people don't mind if you show up late, and a little tipsy.
Odds are they're tipsy too.
They give her extra sick days,
and don't mind if when she calls in
all raspy throated, saying
"I've got the flu."
(Which really means "I'm hung-over.")

She lives in a really rough neighborhood.
I guess she has to.
After all she has been through,
where else could she afford to live?

The worst of the worst show up on her doorsteps.
They take her for all she's got.
She has seen her best friends murdered,
pistol whippings and worse.

Yet, even as hardened a street walker as she is,
even she is shell-shocked.

It would be one thing if she were
to go through this life content with dying
at an early age of cirrhosis,
having her greatest achievement be to take your order from
behind the counter at a Popeye's in Metairie.

But man, you should hear her sing sometime!

In her day she inspired millions.
People still write songs about what a great voice she has.
What grand parties she throws.
What a remarkable cook she is.
And most of all,

how great she looks,
at four in the morning,
wearing nothing,
but voodoo,
and fog.

She does throw a good party though.
She gets all dressed up.
She wears a mask,
so you can't see the dark circles under her eyes.

In the right light, she is exquisite.
She will lure you in.
She'll get you drunk and take advantage of you.

But the next morning,
when you see her without the mask,
make-up all kissed away,
beads lying in the gutter being eaten by rats,
she is sad.

But still somehow, beautiful.

A few years back,
things got really bad for her.
We had to have an intervention.

Had to bring in the cops.
A lot of cops.

We had her on suicide watch.

While she was lying there at her most vulnerable.
She was raped, and left for dead
on the side of the river.
It was tragic. Truly Tragic.

And there are people in this country that actually said,
"She had it comin'. She was askin' for it."

It took weeks, months, years for her to come out of the coma.

Sure some of her friends sent her money,
for a time.

In fact, some came from all over the world,
to sit by her side.
For a time.

But now, things are as bad they ever were,
and no one is ever going to give her
another dime.

Not that I blame them.

She squandered most of the money she was given.
And what she didn't squander,
she was swindled out of.

She has always been so giving,
for someone with such a propensity for trouble.

Now, the sweetest lady in the world
has turned mean.

She is hard.
She carries a gun.
She has a habit.

I'm afraid she has crawled
back inside that bottle,
and even-though the cork has been removed,
she is not coming out.
She simply has no way to grant your wish.

I'm afraid she may stay in that bottle for a long time,
Singin'

Do You Know What it Means, to Miss New Orleans?

But still

I am in love,

with a drunk.

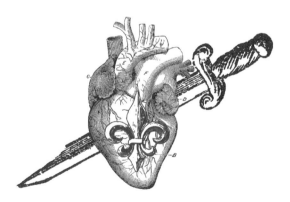

Written in New Orleans in 2008
Originally released on *So, Where ya Headed* (2009)

Thrift Store Diva
(thoughts on fabric #1)

Did you ever stop and think that maybe ...
just maybe ...
there is love?
And there is death...
and there is laundry.....

And that's all there really is.

As for me, my life is a thrift store,
with no walls, no roof.
There's just the moon looking down.

Tonight, she is a thrift store diva
in a silver evening gown.
She is an orb of luscious dust,
all gussied up with borrowed sunlight.

The sun gives the moon all of his gold.
She turns it into silver.
"Unfair, unfair," cried the broken hearts.
She's been short-changing us right from the start.
"Untrue, untrue," the tide objects,
for we only know the moon from the light,
she reflects.

So, as I stand awhile in the isles of merchandise
that have become my life:
A sportsjacket, a necktie.

I came across a set of wings,
that reminds me of the pair
I once had and lost.

They were on display next to

a counter full of broken hearts.

As I fingered the wings, dilapidated down,
a broken heart sighed,

"Without its wings – even the Bird of Paradise himself,
ain't nothin' but a dandified chicken."

To which the wise, well-worn necktie
opened his eyes and replied,

"It's true, I once saw the bird of paradise
without those high falootin wings.
You know where it was?
It was in a Chick Fil-A.

"It was being lowered into a vat of boiling grease.
But it rose, like a mixed metaphor
from its sugary breading,
and turned a midwestern Methodist family of five
into living Pez Dispensers.
They were promptly arrested by mall security
for being uninventoried merchandise,
and are now doing hard time, in a maximum security prison
somewhere beneath Disneyland!"

The sun gives the moon all of his gold.
She turns it into silver.
"Unfair, unfair," cried the broken hearts.
She's been short-changing us right from the start.
"Untrue, untrue," the tide objects,
for we only know the moon from the light,
she reflects.

So needless to say, I purchased that necktie,
(wouldn't you?)
and the sports jacket,
and the set of wings,
and a Pez dispenser with the face of a Methodist.

But I shoplifted the heart,
by placing it in the vest pocket of the sportsjacket.

For I knew
that stolen hearts are better somehow.

And I knew
that I'd be needing this apparel

for my date with the moon...

...and she is already dressed

...and waiting.

By Chris Chandler and Philip Rockstroh
Originally published in *Protection from all this Safety* (1996)
and on the album *Convenience Store Troubadours* (1997)

Victoria

Victoria knows,
that all that I have,
is written on napkins,
and brown paper bags.
But she doesn't care.
She is an island.
She holds me
in the arms of the sea.

Youth and age,
ambition and apathy,
divide us,
like amoebas and galaxies.

Many times, our paths cannot parallel for very long.

As Einstein pointed out,
all straight lines in this round universe,
must intersect.
Which also means,
that once they have intersected,
they are from that point,
forever...   ...diverging.

On this side of the bookend,
I find myself with the same choice
as the other end.
All of my life's story in-between.

I could quit the road, and be rewarded.
With family, community and stability,
and believe me, I have contemplated
all the pros and amateurs
of freedom's
inadequacies.

Victoria knows
that all that I have,
is written on napkins,
and brown paper bags,

held inside a tinderbox,
that flashes like the Hindenburg,
leaving me cowering in fear
of all that is combustible.

Because love is a leaky gas line,
that leaves you dizzy,
and I like to smoke cigarettes after sex.

And if sparks fly,
"Oh, the humanity!"

But Victoria doesn't care.
She is an island.
She holds me
in the arms of the sea.

The Muses are far worse than the tinderboxes.
For the Muse manages to reach into your chest,
and pull out your heart, arteries attached.

You have no choice but to follow,
or the arteries will become detached,
and you will surely die.

You are forced to follow your heart.
Through a darkened wood, deserted street corners,
abandoned parking lots and seedy motel rooms.
Places that you would not normally choose to be, but there you are.

So lost from following the Muse,
that when she finally gives you your heart back,
(which is what Muses do)
you will never find your way home.

She leaves you wishing
you had only paid attention in anatomy class,
so you would have a clue
as to how to put the thing back in.

You stand, heart in hand.
You can feel it throb in your fingertips.
You realize how alone you really are,
with your life – and only your life – in your hands.

For when you follow the Muse,
your life may be all that you will ever have.

Now, as I sit in an alchy bar in Vancouver,
writing on napkins and brown paper bags,
Victoria knows,
that is all that I have.

But she leaves me wishing
she had never taught me
what a Muse really is.

And now my heart is no longer in my hands.

It sits on the bar,
arteries wrapped around my wrists.
One hand clinched to a tumbler full of Jameson,
the other to a pen scribbling on a napkin,
this very poem.

Hoping, that – this time –
what the Muse really had to show me,
was an
anatomy class.

Started in Victoria, BC 1992 and finished in Vancouver, BC 2007
Originally released on the Album *So, Where ya Headed?* (2009)

Winter Poem

Most people think of winter as merely a frozen period.

The poets draw metaphors of death
– the withering away of life,
moving on from the autumn years
into your inevitable demise.

But I say,
"Damn the poets!"

e.e. cummings wrote,
"the snow doesn't give a soft white damn whom it touches"

I always liked that about winter.

Snow makes your weed-infested junkyard
look just as nice as your
Presbyterian neighbor's manicured fescue.

Winter is something you can feel in your bones.

It makes us aware of our skeletal structure,
as it strips the trees of summer,
allowing us to behold the bones of the earth.

We see her landscapes without her
gaudy gardenias and great green summer trees,
her trendy autumn scarves,
or her whorey spring negligees
of tulips and bumble bees.

We see the earth naked –
as we see our lover the next morning.
Make-up kissed away.
The low slant of winter's morning light
reveals the angles of her jaw line.

Down comforters and a sluggish sunrise
let us stay in bed a little longer as we look within.

Some creatures hibernate. For them, winter is gone in a flash.
But it is the cold of winter that gives them the strength
to make it through the rest of the cold-hearted year.

"April is the cruelest month."

It is winter that taught the ant generosity
and the grasshopper responsibility.

(OK, OK – in the original, the ant ate the grasshopper
over the long cold winter –
but I bet the grasshopper learned his lesson.)

George Santayana said,
"To be interested in the changing seasons is a happier state of mind
than to be hopelessly in love with spring."

Perhaps there is a reason that so many people
could not start a conversation with a stranger,
if it were not for the weather.

So, I say,
"God bless the winter."
For it is both an end and a beginning.

It is something that brings us to praise
the hard yellow warmth of chimneys,
as we gather in tighter circles
to hear the tales of the harsher seasons
– until the snow melts,
when we can venture out into the severity of spring
armed with fresh vim
to conquer the oncoming year.

Written in Washington, DC February 2010
Originally released on the album *Matadors* (2012)

She Holds Me In the Arms of the Sea   87

I Always Felt there was No One
I Could Talk About This With

Let them curse our kaleidoscope heart.
We'll snicker through their pastel heaven.
We'll fold our defeats into a defiant hat
and search for shoes to match.

We could shoplift in the finest thrift stores,
and never ask for a pardon,
for the zipper of the seersucker sky is open,
and God loves us so much he has a hard-on.

The thugs of virtue and their riot squads
are after us for this,
and I always felt there was no one
I could talk about this with.

I fell in love with you yesterday,
in the bank, we were standing in line.
The teller must have thought that I had a gun.
I was just depositing a roll of dimes.

She threw her hands up in the air,
screamed and then hit the floor.
Everyone else did the same
though neither of us knew what for.

As we lie in the silence,
unsure if there was a crime,
you smiled, and said you understood when I said,
"I feel like this all the time."

I'm glad to see you understand
why my head's about to split,
and I always felt there was no one
I could talk about this with.

Before I knew that you felt this way,
I had lived a quiet life,
sleeping beneath a manhole cover
unsure of my left from my right.

In my basement workshop,
drawing lines and smoking cigarettes,
I built you an alternative universe,
but I haven't worked the bugs out yet.

Every time I put the finishing touches on the black holes,
I feel that I am done.
Then time starts moving backwards,
and I lose my opposable thumbs.

And so you see I had no choice,
I simply had to quit,
and I always felt there was no one
I could talk about this with.

I tell you this in the strictest confidence,
for I trust that we're both friends.
I went and sat in a laundrymat,
and confessed all of my sins

to an understanding washer and dryer,
and when the rinse cycle fell,
I was absolved, and a nasty gravy stain
was removed as well.

An old man's Rayon shirt cried out,
"How did it come to this?"
and I always felt there was no one
I could talk about this with.

You too heard the rooster crow,
at the brink of kingdom come.
You rolled over and mashed the snooze button,
and we slept through Armageddon.

Armageddon might prove to be a good night,
for you and I to go out.
We could have an intimate evening,
we're sure to avoid the crowds.

If everyone is raptured up to heaven,
we'll get good seats in the theater, they say.
Like when you don't like football,
and it's Super Bowl Sunday.

We'll be on call for the next apocalypse,
but I think I'm gonna call in sick,
and I always felt there was no one
I could talk about this with.

By Chris Chandler and Phillip Rockstroh
Originally published in *Protection from all This Safety* (1996)
and on the album *Collaborations* (1998)

The Last Convent in Gomorrah

The T-shirt factory is working overtime,
since the end of the world has passed.
Everyone wants to advertise
how they survived the blast.
Since it has been determined,
there is no heaven or hell,
noone knows what time it is,
they won't stop ringing those cathedral bells.
That drown the sound of calculators,
trying to cipher the score.
'Til then the mood will be somber,
in the Last Convent in Gomorrah.

Outside, everyone is celebrated
whether they deserve the bow.
Inside, it is no different,
it just seems different somehow.
Joan of Arc is sleeping with a fire-eater
in a wandering minstrel show,
'til attendance at his engagements,
started getting slow.
He's been reduced to begging quarters,
outside convenience stores,
and she went home for Christmas,
to the Last Convent in Gomorrah.

Daniel escaped the lions,
now he has to live with them,
repeating his legend so often
they no longer believe him.
He started off a hero,
he died a drunken man,
playing piano in the brothels,
in the back streets of the promised land.
The lions whisper of conspiracy,

upon the coliseum floor,
as Daniel was placing personal ads.
in the Last Convent in Gomorrah.

Aphrodite claims she's a virgin,
though she dresses quite risqué,
selling overpriced aphrodisiacs
saying, "Don't look at me that way."
She occasionally plays the tambourine,
she bared her breasts on Halloween,
and said everyone who stared at her
was acting obscene.
So they gave her her own radio show,
and now the ratings have begun to soar,
since she started scalping tickets,
to the Last Convent in Gomorrah.

Henry Aaron don't come round no more,
he's playing better than he ever has,
knocking out electric fences,
with an aluminum baseball bat.
He don't return my phone calls,
and for that there is no blame,
I haven't given him sound advice
since he made the Hall of Fame.
He don't need this town no more,
with its heroine and its whores,
but I sure miss the jokes he'd make,
'bout the Last Convent in Gomorrah.

Mae West pretends she's a Buddhist,
since she slept with John Prine.
She agrees with every point of view,
as if it's her on party line.
Her party line she takes to the gallows,
and strings up everyone she meets.
Charlie Chaplin offers up his neck,
and lays down by her feet.
She likes the Queen, and Henry Aaron,
she's met them all before.
She even slept with the fire eater,
in the Last Convent in Gomorrah.

Now, C. – C. C. Ryder,
was finally shown what she had done.
She was forced to stop drinking,
now she don't speak to anyone.
Except of course Jerry Seinfeld,
who is teaching her mandolin,
so that she can start to sing about,
how she's sorry for her sins.
She don't sing the blues no more
she's too busy scrubbing floors,
and tending to the Mother Superior,
in the Last Convent in Gomorrah.

Picasso, he started drinking hard,
ever since he lost his edge.
You can find him at *Katy's Underground*,
on a barstool bowing his head.
I loved him more than all the others,
he gave me room and board,
though he knew I had been banished,
from both Sodom and Gomorrah.
Tuesday left too soon this year,
it was her I did adore,
so I hung the last of the Mardi Gras beads,
in the Last Convent in Gomorrah.

So the calculators are silent,
they don't know who won,
but they know the score,
and the mood is no longer somber…..
… in the Last Convent in Gomorrah.

Written in Hollywood, FL November 1999
Previously unreleased

9th ward, New Orleans #1

Ninth Ward, New Orleans.
With her hollow-eyed men
mumbling on midday benches,
clinging to warm Budweisers,
her sunken sidewalks,
and broken ice-cream trucks,
her rusting bicycles that gallop reckless past
bars on windows, dingy neon, and empty clothes lines,
children barefoot, women pregnant.

You are alive.

Ninth Ward, New Orleans.
With her tattooed boys
banging out chaos on drunken gasoline tanks,
electric scrap metal lies empty in vacant lots,
where all music is experimental,
all experiments have no control,
and no one wonders why nothing is rendered
on canvases made of topless girls,
that spin madness into beauty.

You are alive.

Ninth Ward, New Orleans.
With her shotgun doorways
that open into tiny bars,
filled with sweat and Miller High Life.
Styrofoam plates of silver dollar sausage,
red beans, and plastic forks,
barstools dismembered,
concave linoleum,
and living legends that blow tributes
to departed trumpets until
hollow-eyed men reverberate anew.

You are alive.

Ninth Ward, New Orleans.
With her thick air, and parched water,
her passionate pavement blisters the soulless,
and shoeless black boys ask questions of total strangers.
Where everybody has a hustle,
every hustle has an audience,
and no one really says,
"Good Morning America, How are you?"
Where all movement is slow,
and her exhausted streetcars
still stammer out forgotten desire.

Ninth Ward, New Orleans, you are alive!

Your sunken sidewalks bloom prolific purple.
Invasive beauty buds through your
angry concrete cracking foundations.
Your topless girls pierce the body of night
with jumbled tattoos,
radiant in the mercury vapor twilight.

Your shoeless black boys tap dance
beyond the double-barreled despondent.
Your affluent trumpets hail Gabriel
to come down from his shotgun bar room
and blow new life into this bored bacchanal.

Desire Street is found,
Desire Street is found,
Desire Street is found

in you, Ninth Ward New Orleans.

You are alive!

Written on Desire Street, New Orleans 1995
Originally published in *Protection From All This Safety* (1996)
and on the album *Collaborations* (1998)

Oh Suzanne

You lied.
When you said you were on the pill.
I lied.
When I said it was no cheap thrill.

Did I lie?
When I said I would pay for half.
Did you lie?
When you said you were cool with that?

Oh, Suzanne
Please now don't you cry.
I never could repay you in kind,
You don't recognize
the fear in my eyes
Holding back these tears has left me blind.

The truth is,
I was playing guitar for tips.
The lie is,
You couldn't do more than strip.

The truth is,
it was my biggest mistake.
The lie is,
there was no choice to make.

Here I am in Birmingham,
with a banjo on my knee.
I don't sing this song for you Suzanne,
He would be eighteen.

Oh Suzanne,
Please now don't you cry.
I never could repay you in kind,
You don't recognize the fear in my eyes
Holding back these tears has left me blind.

Previously unreleased. (2009)

Still the Same Song to Me

The words have changed upon the water tower,
in the town where we first met.
It still feels like I'm comin' home,
It's been years since I left.

Play me a song on the guitar,
the one my grandma used to sing.
Though she played it on piano,
It's still the same song to me.

There is a different family on the front porch,
in the house where I grew up,
but that don't mean I'm not the same girl,
that I was when I gave you my love.

Play me a song on the guitar,
the one my grandma used to sing.
Though she played it on piano,
It's still the same song to me.

That old church down on the corner,
Well, it's now a Circle K.
Grandma she was laid to rest there,
I still go down there to pray.

Play me a song on the guitar,
the one my grandma used to sing.
Though she played it on piano,
It's still the same song to me.

Written as a companion to *Sofas and #2 Pencils*
at the High Sierra Music Festival with David Rovics and Samantha Parton in 1996
Originally released on *Convenience Store Troubadours* (1998)

Rings

She had told her daughter to give her a ring.
But the daughter asked,
Why would I give you a piece of jewelry?
No, she said.
Call me.

Still the daughter insisted.
Telephones don't ring, they play songs.

Telephones may play songs,
but they still ring.

They send signals to a satellite
that circles the planet, that orbits the sun,
that loops the galaxy as it rings the universe.

Infinite.
A ring.

Musicians say sound travels in vibrations,
that ripple from its source in waves,
ringing like a pebble thrown in a pond.
It is why bells are said to 'ring.'

Scientists say the universe is shaped like an annulus.

A ring.

All matter exists in the space
between two circles.
One inside the other.
Concentric.

Which is the very definition of a ring.

Poets say our lives are a circle.
May the circle be unbroken.
The circle of life.
The ring of fire.
Sunrise and sun down.

Who are we to argue with
the poets, the musicians, the scientists?

I say, love has entwined our circular lives.
We are now two circles.
Concentric.
One inside another.
An annulus.
The very shape of the universe.

A ring.

So whether there is a piece of jewelry,
or a late night phone-sex telephone ring,
or a song,
or a poem,

or the sad bells of Rhymney ringing,
What did you bring me?

The brown bells of Merthyr will answer,
A hope for the future.

There will always be a ring.

For love has made our lives the shape of the universe.

Infinite.

A ring.

Written in Houston 2010
Originally released on the album *Matadors* (2012)

She Holds Me In the Arms of the Sea   99

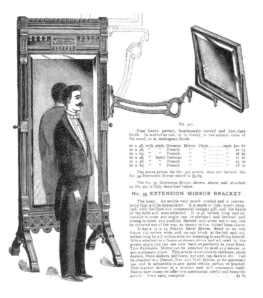

No. 321.

Fine heavy pattern, handsomely carved and first class finish. In walnut or oak, or in cherry, in the natural color of the wood, or in mahogany finish.

20 x 48, with plain German Mirror Plate			...........each	$20 60
20 x 48,	"	"	French	"	"	22 15
20 x 60,	"	"	French	"	"	26 25
20 x 48,	"	"	bevel German	"	"	21 20
20 x 48,	"	"	French	"	"	25 70
20 x 60,	"	"	French	"	"	28 10

The above prices for No. 321 mirror does not include the No. 39 Extension Mirror which is $4 85.

The No. 39 Extension Mirror shown above, and attached to No. 321 is fully described below.

No. 39 EXTENSION MIRROR BRACKET.

The latest. An article very much needed and a convenience that will be appreciated. It is made of iron, nicely ebonized, with the lines and ornamental designs gilt, and the heads of the bolts and nuts nickeled. It is 32 inches long and adjustable to meet any angle; can be elevated and lowered and swung to meet any position desired, and when not in use, can be elevated out of the way, as shown in the dotted lines above.

It has a 14 x 14 French Bevel Mirror, fitted in an oak frame 13½ inches wide, and an oak block at the left end 10½ inches long by 3½ inches wide for fastening to anything desired. When attached to a frame as shown above and adjusted to the proper angle you can see your back as perfectly as your front. This Extension Mirror can be attached to most any mirror, or any stationary place. This article is valuable to clothiers, cloak dealers, dress makers, milliners, hat and cap dealers, etc. Can be attached to a Cheval, Pier and Wall Mirror, or for stationary use, and is adjustable to any point within radius of bracket. This bracket mirror is a wonder and will commend itself. Notice how cheap we offer this substantial, useful and beautiful article. Price each, complete.......................... $4 85

Reflections On
Fun House Mirrors

Reflections of the Hysterical and the Indifferent
(Carnivals #1)

Walking through our urban/suburban landscape
feels like a visit to one of those
roving seedy carnivals of old.

Gaudy, coruscating lights that leave one
feeling queasy, ripped off,
having won only a cheap prize in a rigged game,
that promised something of value,
but was impossible to win.

Step right up!

We have tabloid freak-shows, freeway rollercoasters.
The tattooed lady turns out to be your teenage daughter,
and you are the sucker that paid to get in.

We ride the nine to five Ferris wheels,
and see the forced smiles of phony commercial come-ons,
as distorted as fun house mirrors.

These days, when we look into the fun house mirror,
our reflection seems normal,
for we have grown so grotesque,
that restrooms across America have installed
mirrors from old style carnivals,
while old style carnivals
have installed regular vanity mirrors.

If we were to see an accurate reflection of ourselves we'd say,

"Hey, that guy would have trouble holding a job,
his boss should force him to take a urine test."

An accurate reflection would be invited
to fewer parties and social functions.

William Bennett would write a book
claiming it was the cause of all moral rot.
Moral rot would say it was the cause of William Bennett.
The state of Colorado would propose a referendum,
saying all mirrors with accurate reflections are
no longer protected by the state constitution.

Pat Robertson would claim them to be an emissary of Satan.
Satan would claim he can't comment on the subject,
because he now works for Pat Robertson
and would be forced to take a urine test.

Louis Farrakhan, the Aryan nation, and extremist Arabs and Jews
would all look into this mirror,
and see that their own face,
and the face of their mortal enemy
are the same face.

They would promptly start to hate it, to revile it,
to vainly spend their entire lives
trying to kill their own reflection.

Public opinion polls would show the general public
divided into the hysterical and the indifferent.
24% saying their own reflection was definitely
a threat to all they hold sacred and dear.

17% saying they, themselves, were indifferent
to all they hold sacred and dear.

While the vast majority, 59% had no idea
what they were looking at when they looked in the mirror and
therefore could formulate no opinion.

Madison Avenue carnival barkers will read this data,
park their semis in strip mall parking lots,

and seduce us into
The House of Horrors calling it a Tunnel of Love –
leaving us feeling like you do at Disneyland –
dazed and exploited by some sexless water-fowl
named Donald, and a rodent with a canine pet.

Donald, Mickey, and Pluto have
surgically removed the genitals of the imagination
and imposed the tyranny of the cute.

While a few of us wait for live versions of
William Bennett, Louis Farrakhan and the state of Colorado,
to replace the Disney-like mechanical ones that currently exist,
and lead us in song,

as we sing together in perfect harmony:

"It's a Small Mind After All."

By Chris Chandler and Philip Rockstroh
Originally published in *Protection from all This Safety* (1996)
and released on the album *Convenience Store Troubadours* (1996)

Things Have Never Been the Same

Things have never been the same,
Things Have Never Been The Same.
THINGS have NEVER been THE same.

Not... since the Big Bang.

Not since... the first cosmic gasses cooled into liquid
and vast lifeless oceans began to seethe with DNA
and the seas began to swim with life,
Some of that life didn't like it in the ocean
where its parents lived and thus hauled itself onto the land.
This event caused all the conservative fish
to cry out in alarm at the intrepid lung fish,
"Don't you go and do it. Fish should stay at home!
We live in water. We swim – we don't walk.
We'll lose our very 'fishness' if we're ever caught walking."

Alliances were formed to stop this sort of thing.
Slogans were shaped to fit their purpose:
"Things will never be the same!"
or "Whatever happened to traditional values?"
The Coalition of Concerned Gill-Breathers cried out.
While their paranoid prophet
– a shellfish by the name of Nostradamus
– predicted a dark future of death camps called Red Lobster –
and an evil tyrant named Long John Silver.

Things will never be the same.

Right now – at this very instant –
a sperm cell is fusing with an ovulating egg.

Do they have second thoughts?

Are they are nostalgic for their carefree single days?

Was their intimacy achieved too quickly,
perhaps causing dysfunctional moments to arise?

"Look – I told you that you could move into my womb –
but you moved in and got your DNA all mixed up with mine!
Now, I don't know where you start and I begin.
This is causing me some real problems with my personal boundary issues!"

And that fetus grows into a breathing infant,
and is soon pulled from its mother's breast...
and mother and child will never be the same again....

And let's not ever talk about puberty
(which some claim is a stage of life– but I posit it is more of an affliction.)

For puberty leads us to freedom…
Freedom can be just as daunting as puberty,
and every bit as ugly to witness.

(If you have ever been to an Open Mic Night,
you know what I am talking about.)

Freedom forces me to make choices.

There are so many different religions to choose from.
So many banks, so many kinds of checking accounts,
so many ways to finance an automobile,
so many options on one Ford Taurus…
… So many roads to take,
so many gas stations along each road,
(all with regular, unleaded, super unleaded)
– not to mention varieties of chips on display at the cash register!

SO COME ON!
Which one will it be?
Paper or plastic?

Alright... Let's cut the crap.

We know what we have chosen,
and we will never be the same again....

We sat on the sofa and cast our vote with our remote,
and we became the Republic of Infotania
in the Virtual States of America....

Red, white, and bloodshot eyes
fixed as a blue light flickers revealing a huge, glorious beast.
That beast is everywhere, but exists nowhere.

It has ten thousand mouths that speak at once
and it chatters on and on about power and sex and God
– and, most importantly – delicious salty snacks!

Yet, it provides us not with power, nor sex,
nor allows us to communicate with God,
– but the salty snacks are available just about everywhere.

Millions of years of evolutionary change...
We rose from the oceans' floors...
We prodigal lung-fish should now
return to the water's edge, gloating,

"We are triumphant – we rule the world
– and we bring you –

Pringles!"

Millions of years of evolutionary change...
Yet, we still swim in a vast lifeless ocean of bad news,
shocking tales, and graphic re-enactment....

What do we tell the children?
What do we tell our mangled hearts?
What do we tell the disappointed innocents turned devout cynics?

Tell them, they will never be the same again.

Only the extinct do not change.

So fish and fetus,
suckling infant and sulking cynic.
We may never be the same again,
but this is meant to sound optimistic.

It means simply, we are not stuck this way.

It means we can Change.

It means we will Change.

And it means

we will never be the same again.

By Chris Chandler and Philip Rockstroh
Originally released on the album *Posthumously Live* (2000)
and *Flying Poetry Circus* (2002)

The Ballad of Theodore and His Conspicuous Erection

The first Anthropoid to ever walk erect
was probably having a bad day.
I'll bet his mother said, "Now Theodore,
don't you do that or else you might get stuck that way."

He was a rebel,
didn't give a damn,
He looked her straight in the eye and said,
"Look Ma, no hands."

At school, everybody began to taunt him by saying,
"Theodore, we always did suspect this.
We always thought you to be a Homo...   Erectus...

Theodore is a Homo. Theodore is a Homo."

Soon the word got out
to the ruling class elite,
there was a monkey
who could walk on his feet

They asked, "What's going to happen if this guy
grows a cerebral cortex or an opposable thumb.
We'd be out of a job –
this guy could make us look real dumb."

So as with anything
that challenges the orthodoxy,
the ruling class elite called out the moralists
to fight their war by proxy.

The moralists agreed
and became irate adding,

"The only reason this boy is walking erect
is to proudly display his privates,

and if this keeps up, our civilization
will end in moral defeat.
So the congressional body of monkeys enacted a law
that states we all have to wear a warning label fig leaf."

They condemned this process
of natural selection,
and anything at all to do with Theodore
and his conspicuous erection.

Soon the weirdos, the outsiders saw
how walking erect made the powers that be mad
and it quickly became
a counter-cultural fad.

Soon everybody was talking
about natural selection
and the latest dance craze was
the conspicuous erection.

So the next time you see something
you don't understand
don't dismiss it
with the wave of your hand

If I were you –
I would not be too proud,
for it might be your hairy knuckles
that are dragging the ground.

By Chris Chandler and Philip Rockstroh
originally published in *Protection from all this Safety* (1996)
and on the album *Hell Toupee* (1999)

Freedom Is
(for Blair Powell)

I offered first choice of dueling pistols to an ATM
and I considered it a fair fight.

I missed and hit the little camera above its head,
and the machine cried out with a heavy computer accent,
"Free at last! Free at last! Thank God, I am free at last!"

On the corner I found Freedom
locked inside a 1996 Chevy Malibu.
The safety belt was stuck and she could not exit the vehicle.
She had been trapped there for years
and was barely hanging on to life
sucking substance from miles of abandoned dreams.

I untangled the thin yellow lines from infinite highways
which had ensnared her like cords of Kudzu swallowing power-lines
on an Alabama backroad.

I bought her a tank of gas and together we took off.

I can't say for sure, but I think we did doughnuts in the parking lot
for ten years until we ran out of gas.
The only thing I know for sure is that when she finally stopped,
we were in the same gas station parking lot and
Freedom had not changed a bit.

She left me there.
Dizzy.
Alone.

I was without Freedom
and forced to fill out a missing persons report.
The cops reluctantly wrote down my description as I said.
"Freedom no longer has a full tank of gas."

...a full tank of gas.

...glancing in the mirror and not noticing yourself.

...winning a contest and spending all of the prize money on the runners up.

...waxing your moustache into a Salvador Dali to let small children play with the curlicues.

...giving credit to the space as one of the letters in the alphabet.

...premature reincarnation.

...a blank yellow legal pad sitting on the driver's seat of a $250 pick up truck - sold as is.

FREEDOM IS

...thanking a god you don't believe in

...recognizing the wanton glint in a stranger's eye

... gathering strangers for a chorus of: "NO MORE CHANTING!"

BY: CHRIS CHANDLER

...getting your tongue stuck on the frozen metal while giving a blow-job to a bronze statue of the city's fathers because they need one so.

...a vice.

...a slave to want. ...drawing underarm hair on advertisements – then thanking the ad company for printing them that way. **...a virtue.**

...filling eleven pages in the yellow legal pad found on the driver's side seat of a $250 Pickup.

...using the word blow-job so that your list of platitudes will not wind up printed on a poster hanging in the bath room of an insurance salesman living in the suburbs of a minor American city.

...free from want

...obeying traffic lights you see on TV.

...making eye contact with the blind.

...giving your hat to a total stranger just because she looks good in it.

...dancing in public.

...dancing alone.

...dancing with strangers.

...having hard feelings.

...dancing with your lover.

...taking those hard feelings, tying them to a stick, then using it as a hammer to build a cathedral for the one that made you feel that way.

...dancing with your mother.

...dancing with your ex.

...mispelling.

...coffee black when on the run - with cream &...

...sugar at sunset.

a road-side diner - open all night.

...tipping well when you can't afford it.

& not pursuing it...

The cop interrupted me and said,
"No, what does she look like?"
I said, "Freedom is glancing in the mirror and not noticing yourself."

She is a blank yellow legal pad sitting on the driver seat
of a $250 pickup truck, sold as is.

On a cold day, Freedom is
getting your tongue stuck on the frozen metal
while giving a blowjob to a bronze statue of the city's fathers
– just because they need one so.

Freedom is
using the words 'blowjob' so that your list of platitudes will not wind up
printed on a poster hanging in the bathroom of
an insurance salesman living in the suburbs of a minor American city.

Freedom dances with strangers.
She is dancing alone.
She is dancing with your lover.
Dancing with your mother.
Dancing with your ex.

Freedom is tipping well when you can't afford it.

...is waxing your mustache into a Salvador Dali
and letting small children play with the curly cues.

...is drawing underarm hair on advertisements hanging in the subway,
then writing a letter to the ad company thanking them
for printing the ads that way.

Freedom is premature reincarnation.

...is making eye contact with the blind.

The cops looked confused until I spotted her out of the corner of my eye
gathering a group of pedestrians for a rousing chorus of

"No more chanting! No more chanting! No more chanting!"

Freedom is
thanking a God you don't believe in.

...Is losing a contest, shaking the hand of the winner,
looking them in the eye and saying, "No hard feelings."

...Is having hard feelings.

...Is taking those hard feelings and tying them to a stick
so that they can be used as a hammer
to build a cathedral for the one that made you feel that way.

...Is obeying stop lights you see on TV.

...Is giving credit to the space as one of the letters in the alphabet.

Eventually the cops got frustrated, and wandered off
in the direction of the crowd that had gathered still yelling
"No more chanting!"
The cops joined in while arresting them all for civil obedience.

Last I heard she is still in county lockup
somewhere north of the Macon County line.
I visited her once, though I am not convinced she recognized me.

Though fifteen years had passed – her trial had still not come up
and no one had posted bail.

She offered me a dueling pistol and pointed me towards an ATM.

I considered it a fair fight.

Written at Eddie's Attic, Atlanta 2004
Originally released on the albums
Live from the Wholly Stollen Empire (2005) and *Matadors* (2012)

WHOOP
(please step away from the vehicle)

I found my inner child,
but someone else's inner child
beat him up and stole his lunch money.

I saw my missing humanity
on the back of a milk carton
and noticed the expiration date had passed.

I long for that feeling of security
when I step from my brand new vehicle
and the closing of the door makes that sound . . .
. . . safe.

You know, I bet somewhere out there
it's somebody's job to make a new car sound that way.
When you close the door. . .
. . . safe.

The car alarm only adds to the experience . . .
. . . Whoop.

Sometimes I think I need a bigger Whoop. . .
. . . WHOOP.

Yet still, I have this nettling dread
that somewhere out there. . .
there are angry, underclass, urban black people
that want to steal my lawn furniture.

We need more security.

We need more cops on the streets.
Higher walls.
More bars on windows.

We need more handguns.
We should be able to carry concealed weapons
– but ONLY WE should be able to carry them.
We need more bulletproof vests.
We need more therapists.

We need more driver-side airbags.
We need more passenger-side airbags.
We should have pedestrian air bags.
We need more vigilant right-winged talk show hosts.
I need a better car alarm.

Whoop! Please step away from the vehicle.

We need more urine tests.
We need more latex.
We need more tamper-proof packaging.
We need more wax on fruit.
We need more DDT,
....no, less DDT.

Whoop! Do not penetrate the shrink wrapped vegetables.

We need more plastic surgery to protect us from time itself.
Time is a thief,
and I want to see it number one on America's Most Wanted.
Time should not be allowed
to speed up during moments of excitement,
nor to slow down during moments of tedium.
Time should be ordered to arrive on time.

In the remote chance that a snowball
ever does have a chance in Hell,
heads should roll.

That's what the law *should* say, and we need more laws!
We need tougher and more mandatory sentencing laws.
We need more prisons.
We need more death penalty statutes.

We need more electric chairs.
Hell, we should have electric sofas.
We should have electric dining room sets.
A lethal injection happy hour, two for the price of one.
And an all you can eat hemlock salad bar and buffet.
We should banish all uncertainty.

All spontaneous utterances
should be memorized in advance.

Whoop! Please step away from the vehicle.

All flights of the imagination
should be grounded and searched for dangerous and smuggled cargo.

Whoop! Please step away from the vehicle.

All monsters should remain under the bed
and not fraternize with skeletons in the closet.

Whoop! Please step away from the vehicle.

Whoop, protect me –
whoop Whoop, WHOOP, PROTECT ME!!!

I have a vial of Prozac® in one hand
and a handgun in the other.

MY THERAPIST IS A CARD CARRYING MEMBER OF THE NRA.

STOP!!!!!!!!!!

Is that what this country was founded on?

Wasn't this country founded by people
who were willing to sail across the known horizon
in search of unknown land?

It was the risk-takers that went.

The meek ones stayed back in Europe saying,
"You guys go ahead, really I wanna come
– but I just want to finish this last Victor Hugo novel.
We'll be along as soon as you get settled,
as soon as you tame the wilderness
– as soon as you get cable."

So they went,
and this country was founded on the spontaneity of thievery.
But today, it is only the thievery that remains.

We are run by demagogues who run on campaign promises
that say they can make the trains run on time.
But don't you see,
that's the point,
the trains are not supposed to run on time!

We're supposed to hang out in train stations,
looking at total strangers,
making eye contact with total strangers. . .

. . . falling in love
with total strangers.

What we need is protection.

Protection, from all this...

...safety.

By Chris Chandler and Philip Rockstroh
Originally released on the album *Generica* (1995)
and *Protection from all this Safety* (1996)

On Playing George Bush

Whenever I try to really understand a problem,
I try to put myself in the other guy's shoes
- like an actor would.

An actor who plays a villain,
does not see himself as a villain.

He finds some pretext to justify his actions.

With that in mind,
how do you play George Bush?

Even the worst community theatre thespian,
would find it to be like
Lawrence Oliver trying to play Dobie Gillis.

His own motivations seem skewed.

OK, we all know this Iraqi debacle
had nothing to do with
The World Trade Center.
Maybe it had something to do with world trade,
but not *The World Trade Center.*

At best, it was to try and install an
American-friendly government into the Middle East.
(which is kind of like asking
Michael Jackson to babysit your kids.)

Everyone knew that
Saddam's army was a paper tiger.
(Well, more like one of those origami cranes.)

We knew we could have American troops
in Baghdad in a matter of days.

American military intelligence
is not so bad that it REALLY thought
a second-rate dictator had
hijacked the set of a James Bond movie,
and was ready to use its mobile crystal meth labs
to contaminate Ft Knox.

That wasn't the objective.
We know that.
We knew it then,
and we know it now.

However, there was no plan for what to do
AFTER their military took off its uniform.

There are all kinds of examples in history
that he could have learned from,
to make a defeated country
accept its new status as a franchise.

To do that, you would have
to know something
about history.

I think it is pretty obvious,
that George Bush never attended
a history class when he went to Yale.
Maybe when he got his honorary degree
at Bob Jones University,
but not at Yale.

After Lee surrendered at Appomattox,
in the few days he had left on this earth,
Lincoln did something brilliant,
that George Bush could have learned from.

He made sure
that the surrendering army
would continue getting paid.

He took their arms, and sent them home.
Told them to tend to their families.
He gave them benefits
as if they were Union army veterans.

It helped to unify a country torn apart by civil war,
and was a hell of a lot cheaper
than continuing to police
a hostile, economically devastated country.
(Sound familiar?)

So, what I want to know is...

Once we got to Baghdad...

Where were the aircraft carriers filled with cement mixers,
and the skies looking like Normandy,
only filled with parachutes dropping generators
made in Normal, Illinois?

Where were the battalions of construction workers?
Where were the divisions of translators and cultural liaisons?
Where were the brigades of electrical and civil engineers?

Surely, they weren't busy in New Orleans.

Why the HELL didn't Enron
step up to help fix the power grid,
instead of declaring bankruptcy?
Why have we still not fixed the power grid?

You bomb it, you fix it.

Hindsight is only 20/20
when you have some sort of vision to begin with.

The past four years we have had Mr. Magoo
sailing the ship of state off the edge of the flat earth.
"Oh Magoo, you've done it again."

We have lost the moral high-ground.

Anyone with any military training knows,
that once you've lost the high-ground,
it is nearly impossible to retrieve.

Right now, this looks like Pickett's charge,
with George Bush looking every-bit as presidential
as Larry the Cable Guy shouting,

"Stay the course... Get 'er done!"

We have a doomed cause...
with NO CHANCE of taking back the moral high-ground,
and we are now in full retreat.
And anyone who has ever studied military tactics
should see that.

But wait a second...
No-one in the Bush administration
HAS a military background.

Their idea of a military background,
is a flight suit,
and an aircraft carrier,
from which to hurl John Wayne-isms.

"Mission Accomplished?"

There are those out there that say,
that this guy is so bad,
that you can't compare him
to another American presidency.
"Worst President ever," I hear.

I say, "Not so!"

I compare him to...
Jefferson Davis.

An American President who came from privilege,
who was NOT elected,
and whose cause was morally bankrupt.
Yet he had no problem sending thousands
of young Americans to fight and die for it.

So, if we do as our President says,
why aren't we showing real faith in the Iraqi government
by pulling out of there?

Why aren't we trying the perpetrators
of Hadifa and Abu Ghraib in an Iraqi civilian court?
Why aren't we watching these events
unfold on International Court TV?
WHERE IS JUDGE MOHAMMED WAPNER WHEN YOU NEED HIM!?

So which is it?
Do we believe in the new Iraqi Government or don't we?

If we do,
we should pull out,
and let them run their own lives.

If we don't,
we should pull out.
It is clear we are impeding the process of a stable government.

Either-way,
we should pull out.

Admit our mistakes honestly, openly.
Forgive ourselves. Ask for forgiveness.
and maybe the world will begin to forgive us too.

After-all, what WOULD Jesus do?

Written in Washington, DC 2004
Originally released on the album *American Storyteller Volume III* (2005)

Credit History

So I was wrestling with this demon....

Well, he really wasn't a demon per say,
he was just real annoying.

And we weren't exactly wrestling,
I was kinda dodging his phone calls.

But, they were real annoying phone calls,
from this figure straight out-a Hell.

Well, not exactly Hell.
He was from a collection agency.

You see, I purchased salvation on my credit card.
Well, not exactly salvation.
but close.

I purchased on my credit card
five hundred dollars worth of books on
self improvement,
miracle diets,
and books on angels.
Not to mention
the added expense of a really
comfortable reclining chair to seek
salvation upon.

I'm comfortable with the fact that
a comfortable chair
allows me to be comfortable,
reading these books
that teach me to be comfortable
with myself.

Some soul-numb skeptics
might deride the fact that I have
charged hundreds of dollars in take-out pizza
during this period of self-improvement.

How else could I not properly absorb
all the information in my diet books,
if I am too hungry to concentrate.

This, after all, is a battle for my soul.
Or at least as important
– my credit rating.

Which is infinitely intertwined
with my feelings of self worth,
which is infinitely intertwined
with my need for self-help books,
which is infinitely entwined
with my credit rating,
which is...
Well... You get the point.

I simply had to charge this book on my
LORD & MASTER CARD.

Since when is the Higher Power concerned with diet books?

When was he not?

He has convinced the Jews to stay Kosher,
the Muslims to stay clear of swine,
the Protestants to add mayonnaise to everything.

So the way I see it, the Higher Power
can certainly inspire a best-selling diet book.

Which gets us back to
my holy war with the credit agency.
They claim that my entire life's story

is on file in their computer.
My entire life story has come to this.
A few electronic flashes of light...
a billion angels dancing on the head of a micro chip.
(Now that is some diet they're on to be able to do that!)

But where does it get off claiming that I, am a deadbeat!
I want to tell that computer
to mind its manners, and watch what it
says about me in public.
If I ever saw that smug son of a mother-board...
I'd call it out... but you can't...
you can't fight what you can't see...

You just flail into the empty air.
Like taking a swing at the Gods themselves.
Only the way I see it,
the corporations are the Gods.

They are faceless allusive entities
that speak in cryptic slogans and symbols...
called logos....
You won't even know they are there,
until they are hitting you up with
the corporate collection plate.

Today even Zeus would fall,
overwhelmed and defeated before
The Great God Walmart.

The Gods aren't dead;
they're just out shopping.

Aphrodite bought a nitey at Victoria's Secret,
while Eros joined a recovery group for sex addiction.
He traded his bow and arrows
in a sporting goods department for a 9 mm.
and was last seen heading to a high school in the deep south
(to start an NRA Gun Safety Club of course.)

Now Jesus – He's learned the score.
He has learned from his years of hanging around
the wretched and poor, that
there is a better way to market to us.
He's opened a Mega-Church,
named Saved-Mart.
His plan is to open one in every town in the USA,
and put those pitiful, main street churches
out of business for good.

He's not just the Son of God – He's the CEO!

For God so loved the world – He bought the company!

Oh father, please forgive me...
....for my credit rating...
...as I forgive those who have bounced checks to me.

Yea though I walk
through the valley of the shadow of
too many inquires and a poor debt to credit ratio
– I would fear no evil.

IF I JUST HAD A BETTER CREDIT RATING.

In the meantime – I'll settle for some TV
and the holy deliverance of take-out pizza

– ON EARTH AS IT IS IN HEAVEN.

By Chris Chandler and Philip Rockstroh
Originally released on the albums *Hell Toupee* (1999)
and *Flying Poetry Circus* (2003)

Fast Food Confederacy

Who said slavery has been abolished?
Seems to me the rules were only polished.

Polished like the formica and chrome,
at the Ronald McDonald Plantation Burger Home.

Seems to me that things have remained pretty much the same.
What's the difference between outright slavery
and four dollars and some change?

In the indentured service industry,
there is a new slaveship conspiracy,
The Fast Food Confederacy.

They have been plottin'
something rotten.
Burgers are the new cotton,
in the Fast Food Confederacy.

At least they gave the slaves free housing
in the fields of the southern confederation,
but these days they keep the quarters so far out of sight,
they have to be bussed into the suburban plantation.

Where they take their positions behind the cash register
– you ever notice they got pictures of the menu
– right their on the keys?
Like in the old south,
they still don't teach slaves how to read.

They have replaced the heat of the Mississippi sun,
for a hot grill and a sesame seed bun.
I don't know what's going to cure this evil.
What we need 'bout now
is a sesame seed boweevil.

In the indentured service industry,
there is a new slave ship conspiracy,
The Fast Food Confederacy.

They have been plottin'
something rotten.
Burgers are the new cotton,
in the Fast Food Confederacy.

Over at Domino's Pizza,
it's to the right to life movement,
that your dollar does pay.
They wanna make sure everything gets delivered
so they can breed them a new crop of slaves.

Kentucky Fried Chicken is the only one that is honest,
but I won't say brave.
At least Colonel Sanders,
looks like he owns slaves.

Oh, but they're not slaves,
they could always quit.
But, homelessness is as cruel
as the crack of the Foreman's whip.

For singing this song
I might get lynched by a mob
over at the Circle K... K.K.
But don't give me no tombstone
just put the golden arches
over my Chick McGrave.

By Chris Chandler and Philip Rockstroh
Originally released on the album (Cassette) *A Funny Thing Happened on the Way to the Abyss*
(1990), released on *As Seen on NO TV* in 1992, on the album *Flying Poetry Circus* 2002,
and published in the book *Protection From All this Safety* (1996)

Sex, Sex, Sex

What I want to know is,
why the Christian Coalition
can't stop thinking about other people's
genitalia?

Usually that's how we define a pervert:
someone who can't keep their mind off of
Sex sex sex.

But, that's all these guys think about.

Ralph Reid, Pat Robertson, Jerry Falwell,
I'm flattered and all,
but could you please, please, please
get your heads out of my pants?

Hell, I had to quit going to church
just so i could stop hearing about sex all the time!

You guys could walk past a hungry, uneducated child,
drive across a polluted city, crumbling with neglect,
and not miss a beat saying,
"All the world's problems are caused because
somebody was thinking too much
and too often about other people's
genitalia."

For once, you're right.
Those people are you.

You really should start thinking of something else.
Maybe if you just
did it more, and thought about it less,
you'd stop being so obsessed with the subject.

And maybe,
if you thought about it less,
and did it more,
you would worry less about
who I could marry in this country.
And a little more about who this country can kill.

You remind me of when we were in high school,
we would lay awake at night
scrutinizing the discovery of masturbation,
dreaming of encounters of
sex sex sex.

But if we happened across a girl
that was the least bit promiscuous
we called her:
slut slut slut.

All us pubescent boys, at home alone,
pulling and pawing at our little chubbies –
trying to turn them in to full-blown woodies
by fantasizing about the very same women
that by day we disparaged.

Now Jerry Falwell,
I'm touched that you are laying awake at night thinking of me,
(and probably touching yourself)
but would you please try and say
nicer things about me during the day.

Maybe this is why so many fundamentalist preachers
get caught in cheap motel rooms, pants round their ankles,
disgraced in the company of hookers
with unfortunate complications and fire-sale prices.

These crypto-puritans might as well
shake their fingers at trees
for dropping pollen on car windshields
and into our sinus cavities.

"Oh, how it penetrates me against my will.
I think this is grounds for sexual harassment."

It's ridiculous.
You can just see trees on Oprah saying
"It wasn't my fault.
We swear by our roots, branches, and leaves
it wasn't our idea.

"We were victims,
the victims of bees.
They're sneaky, persistent, aggressive,
all they eat is sugar,
it makes them hyperactive –
they should be put on Ritalin.

"You know they are dysfunctional.
They live with their mothers all their lives,
(absent fathers and all...)
all they do is roam the country,
looking for trouble,
sex on their minds

"In and out they fly,
in and out.
Their hot little wings
beating briskly around our hot little petals.
They're sticking their tongues in our open flowers.
The sun touching my tender new leaves.
Winter's rigidity falling away.
My sap rising.

"The sun just watched – the old voyeur
He should be held as an accessory.
Notice it didn't call the authorities,
it didn't call the Christian Coalition.

"It is rumored after all that
the sun itself was formed by the big bang.

A sort of cosmic one night stand."

All the universe thinks about is:

Sex sex sex.
But it was God
that created the flowering earth
and the salacious, sensuous stars,
and you
and me,

Since our address is the universe
we too think about:
Sex sex sex

So on Judgment Day,
I will gladly take my chances,
because I feel The Creator
will be much more tolerant of those of us,
who have erred on the side of
Eros –
than those who have slept with
Hypocrisy,
in the pursuit of power.

By Chris Chandler and Philip Rockstroh
Originally published in *Protection from all this Safety* (1996)
and on the album *Convenience Store Troubadours* (1997)

Angry Young Man

He was an angry young man.
Was an angry young man.
But he soon grew out of it.
Became an angry middle-aged man,

He was an angry middle-aged man.
Was an angry middle-aged man.
"Cause he never had a wife, never made any friends,
when he was an angry young man.

Became an angry old man,
Walkin' down the street muttering to himself.
Takin' his time in the crosswalk.
"Cause he didn't wanna play shuffleboard.

Now, he's an angry dead man.
Left an angry epitaph.
Which read:
"He was angry that he wasted his life.
As an angry young man".

Written In New Orleans 1995
Originally released on the album *Convenience Store Troubadours* (1997)

The Split Second
Between when the
Trapeze Artist Flies
and She Grasps
the Hand of Her Catcher

Matadors

Understand...
        ...that this entire poem...
                ...takes place in a split second...

Which is to some an eternity,
such as the split second between when a trapeze artist takes flight
and she grasps the hand of her catcher.

"Ladies and Gentlemen,"
I thought to myself,
but the words just wouldn't come.

One-hundred-thousand times before, the words have flown freely
– but not this time…

I fumbled in the front pocket of my red velvet jacket
and pulled out my notes… yep that's what it says alright –
"Ladies and Gentle…"
The words would not come.

I peeked through the closed curtains
and peered into a sea of dull faces waiting to be entertained.
Their empty eyes glinting like the lights of a ship
viewed from beneath the water.

Fish cannot see above the water.
Occasionally they can make out movements, gestures,
even danger above the water… sometimes…
on a clear day… they will gather in a school to watch…
for they know there is a thin line
between their water and our air
where another world is possible.

For as Einstein pointed out:
"Reality is merely an illusion, albeit a very persistent one."

Perhaps the thin line between them is a red velvet curtain.

A performer on a bright stage cannot see into the darkened audience,
but he knows there is another world out there.
The audience does too.
Like a school of fish, it is why they came.

Performer and audience must work together
to lift the veil between the worlds known and unknown
to prove to the world that another way is possible.

Only a red velvet curtain exists between us.
That curtain must go up.

The house lights go to half.
The words still will not come, yet I know I must dive in.

I do so...
          ... but I realize…
                         ...I cannot swim.

But I see a school swims together in perfect unison,
like aerial fliers, knowing no gravity except that of their camaraderie
and their desire for spectacle.
Flips and turns and loopty-loops and unpredictable pirouettes.
But it is my turn to fly freely – to add my component to the presentation –
but the words would not come.

The stage manager is backstage with a hook.

In Terror I break from the school.
Swimming. Alone. Hungry.
Eyeing a silver spinner – I am thinking, "It's dinner time!"
but, as soon as I bite – out of the blue –
a magic string sucks me from the known universe.

Suddenly, I am lying on the deck of a boat – floundering.
There are aliens wearing bright orange vests and baseball hats
that read things like, "Who farted?"

I am unable to breathe in the alien's atmosphere.
All seems lost.   The lights continue to fade.

The red velvet curtain rises...

A polite applause sputters and dies out
leaving me with an uncomfortable silence…

A full five minutes passes – the silence turns to heckles.
Fruit flies freely.
I am floundering. I am floundering.

I remove my jacket to use it as a shield to dodge the fruit
but somewhere in an alternative universe
a bull sees it as a signal to charge.
There is a large swelling of applause from the empty ocean.
It gives me confidence.

Perhaps it is applause that allows one to defy gravity.
They are cheering loudly.
And then I realize...
                    ...they are rooting for the bull.

Yet, I don't care that they are rooting for the bull!
At least they are cheering…

For tonight, I must be *Myro the Magnificent*,
the heralded, undisputed, undefeated greatest Matador of all time…

Then I have the sinking revelation that the bull really is charging...
                    ..and that all LIVING matadors are undefeated.

The Stage manager has set down her hook
and replaced it with a butterfly net.
I am floundering on the deck.
The aliens scoop me into a net and toss me back into the water,
where I witness the tiniest of tiny minnows performing
a beatific ballet for the audience of much larger fish
in an effort to convince it that they are indeed enormous

(which is not unlike the reason that
insecure performers immolate themselves for approval.)

I try to join them – but now,
I am just that old guy with a hook in my mouth
trying to convince the school that there is an alternative universe.

Naturally, they don't believe me.
They put me on a reality TV show and I find myself
trying to convince some blowfish named Bill O'Reilly,
that I was abducted by aliens.

I am a laughingstock – but at least – they are laughing…
Because, when they are laughing, I CAN FLY!

There are many ways for us to convince the world
that there is another way possible.
There is a world beyond the dreary theatre seats
and boxes of stale greasy popcorn.

And that world can be found in a split-second.

It is a split-second in which we all can fly…
One in which fish can walk…
One in which the bull dons a red cape and trades his horns for a sword.
One in which the bird is free from the chains of the sky….

The curtain is up!

I hear the applause, and I realize that I am right…
that THIS is the alternative universe….

This is the split second between when the trapeze artist flies
– and she grasps the hand of her catcher…

Which is the split second between two hands clapping.

Written at the Oregon Country Faire 2010
Originally released on the album Matadors 2012

American Idle

"I have seen the best minds of my generation..."
writing ad copy.

Tonight as I drown my sorrows in a beer ad,
I think of Eliot, of Yeats and Molière –
what would they have made of it all?

I wonder if they would be today's poets
– the ones writing
"This Bud's for you,"
"I love you, man,"
and it don't get no better than this?"
You know, the classics?
Or would they be writing the TV shows themselves?

Would they write
"What biggest loser
slouches down project runway
waiting to be lost."

Would they be sitting at the right hand of God.
That's the one where He holds the remote control.

Since the moment that God said,
"Let there be light."
And he hit the universal remote,
and the first little white dot appeared
on the giant surround sound television screen in the sky,

And Adam and Eve sat down
– in their little fig-leaf bathrobes,
on their little Fred Flintstone couches
to watch God's first mini-series,
known as *The Constellations*.
And those stories danced in their dreams.

And were passed on, until they got to us,
and we're so twisted we watch
Dancing with the Stars.
In fact, *The Constellations* were the
longest-running show in human history –
longer than *The Guiding Light*, longer than *The Simpsons*,
longer than one of Jay Leno's monologues.

But *The Constellations* got cancelled by a new show called *Smog*.

So now people go to sleep watching shows like *American Idol*
where the premise is for
the people to become "stars" that no longer exist!

But our definition of star has become as distorted
as our view of the night-time sky in downtown Los Angeles.

Why do you think every body in LA wants to be a star?
'Cause there are no stars!

But people fall asleep watching that crap –
heavily medicated, probably involving a creepy butterfly
that flies into your room and takes you to play chess with Abraham Lincoln,
and a talking Gopher and a mute guy in an antique diving bell
Until you wake up - mid afternoon - literally in a threesome with Bob Barker
and Drew Carey after a mysterious stranger shouting "Come on Down!"

And you notice that *Jiffy Pop Popcorn* and *Johnson Floor Wax*
retails for the same amount of money.
And for noticing that innocuous anomaly,
you are asked to spin a giant Catherine Wheel,
that looks as if it belonged to Liberace himself
– until you find your self shouting,
"The price is NOT right!"

Even though the price is NOT right
– we worship our entertainers – as long as they're famous.
It is not like the days of the bard –
where the wondering minstrel strolled from township to town,

campfire to campfire
singing the stories of the village just over there
– long before they were written down.
Stories like the Bible, the Torah and the Qurán,
And didn't all these warn us
about worshipping at a false American Idol?

And the famous?
They'll do anything to stay famous.
They'll go on talk shows to talk about
how hard it is to be famous.
How hard it is to be on the road.
And they'll stab each other in the back
to take jobs as insipid game show hosts,
or judges on contests that make
no talents... famous.

So I say, "Fame is for sissies!"

Hell, It would be easy to be on the road for twenty-five years
if you were famous.
Doing one night stands. Staying in hotel rooms. Hot showers, Meals.

Try doing it for twenty-five years
when you're passing the hat in a coffeehouse in North Dakota!

It's true with anything you love.
And it's not just about fame.
You may be the best widget-maker in the world
– and no one notices.
So the guy in the assembly line next to you gets the promotion.
And you still have to find a way to keep being
the best widget-maker in the world.

The only way to do that,
is to keep being the best widget-maker in the world
And tell stories about being the best widget-maker…
to your kids.

Written in New York City in 2008
Originally released on the album *So, Where ya Headed?* (2009)

Last Thoughts on Elvis Presley

Ascending skywards, in a glass elevator,
whose path through the clouds runs along the outside
of a cathedral of corporate capitalism.
Hymns of devotional Muzak fill the vessel:
Simon and Garfunkel, Huey Lewis, Elvis Presley.

Elvis.

From that vantage point, the city was luminous beneath me.
All those lights, electric lights, neon lights, fluorescent lights
that beaded into a mosaic of votive candles.

It was glorious.

It was the glorious, glinting of the
jewel-studded celestial jumpsuits
of ten thousand Elvis imitator angels
doing a command performance for God.

As I reached the 70th or 75th floor, my ears began to pop,
for I was so close to God that I could actually hear him count his money.

And I wondered how this glass elevator could ever be
a chariot coming forth to carry me home...
when the only home I've known is *The Home Shopping Network*.

Perhaps that's why the epiphany arrived.
with the crystalline clarity of a world of Zirconium Diamonds,
resplendidly reflecting a thousand fluorescent suns.

You see, we are like Elvis... in the 70s.

Puffy and bloated, wheezing our way through our set,
heaving our way across the world stage.
The fans still scream for more, failing to notice any decline.

The world wants what we have,
but America has left the building.

America died like Elvis,
retching pharmaceutical cocktails into the toilet.

Our culture died,
but its imitator is sporadically spotted
at Burger Kings and Walmarts.
First it was in Gallup, New Mexico,
but then in the Kentucky Fried Chicken
adjacent to the Eiffel Tower, and in the 7-11
reflected in the pools outside the Taj Mahal.

Our Culture is sequinned across the global landscape.
All those lights, electric lights, neon lights, fluorescent lights
– visible even from space.

Our globe shines like one of Elvis' Las Vegas costumes,
but no one sees the dying man beneath the jeweled jumpsuit.

The Gods that once dwelled in nature,
now dwell in culture,
and even our culture of excess...
....must have a God.

So I guess glittering Elvis is the God of it all.

He rises from the ashes everywhere,
in every flashing or blinking running light,
every strobing fluorescent tube light,
glimpsed in every glowing sign,
atop every home-delivery pizza truck
on Earth.

We await the Elvis Pentecost,
when it will rain triple cheeseburgers,
fried peanut butter and banana sandwiches,
and Percodans from Heaven!

Our guarded gated communities
are our own personal Graceland.
Behind its walls we die
of isolation and excess.

The land and the king are one.
He is the gleaming God of the millennium's end.

Did we dream Elvis

or did Elvis dream us?

Dreaming?

By Chris Chandler and Philip Rockstroh
Originally released on the album *Generica* (1995),
Published in *Protection from All This Safety* (1996)
and *Convenience Store Troubadours* (1997)

Top Banana

A man, down-on-his-luck, has been hired to stand in front the entrance to a
car wash – wearing a gorilla costume – as a marketing ploy of the owner to
promote business.

Now, this unfortunate man had not foreseen his life coming to this.
He had not approached a table on career day in high school manned
by a guy wearing a gorilla costume and surrendered to his true destiny.

He had been a rising star in his chosen field, a trader in commodities....
One of those wildly gesturing, hyper-adrenaline types you see on
the floor of the commodities market
(which I like to think of as the mosh-pit of the corporate world.)
His voice had been his secret of success: It was loud but resonant;
a baritone that rose above the shrill piping of the others.

Then one day his voice just gave out. Tragically, he could not be heard above
the din as he rasped out,

"BUY BRAZILIAN BEEF FUTURES!"

He was misunderstood to have said,

"BUY ASIAN SEA CUCUMBERS!"

And he was completely wiped-out in a financial panic
stemming from an epidemic of Mad Asian Sea Cucumber Disease.

Down the block, the owner of a competitive car wash
takes note of the gorilla costume gambit, and is forced into action.

An auto parts calendar model is hired.
(in fact – she was the actual – in the flesh – Miss Ball-Bearing, July 1989)
She adorns the entrance of the driveway clad only in a bikini.
Perhaps Beauty can beat back the Beast.
And indeed what American can resist sex and shiny cars.

Business soars.

Back up the street, this fact is quickly grasped.
Measures must be taken.
The gorilla is given a pith helmet and a whip,
and one, Mistress Doris – a paralegal/ part-time dominatrix
– is signed to team with the gorilla.

Plus the name of the business is changed from
Reliable Wax & Wash to *The Marquis de Suds*.

The new slogan: *We don't just clean filth – We humiliate it*.

These developments do not go unnoticed by the local clergy
– who convince adolescents in their youth groups,
to gather buckets, sponges and garden hoses.
They offer a free car wash (or a vehicular baptism– as they call it in the trade)
for every conversion – plus a free lube job and tire rotation
for frequent church attendance.

A minister was heard to say,
"If Jesus was here today – he would have to wash more than just feet
to compete."

But back down at the *Marquis*,
the outward trappings of success have changed the man in the gorilla outfit.
He's tasted fame.
Perhaps, the sound of the approving car horns have gone to his head.
But he wants something more – not simply more shallow acclaim,
mind you – he wants to expand creatively.
He does not want to limit himself to roles that entail wearing animal suits...

There was the possibility of landing the role of
Abe Lincoln at *Honest Abe's Log Cabin Mobile Home & Winnebago*.

It seems the soul inside the man inside the hairy suit
must reveal itself at long last....
And he just knew he shared this yearning with
his fans and admirers out there in the traffic.

He knew that they, like him,
long to remove the mask they wear at work
– to shed the silly suit, and to be loved for their true selves.

But, of course, to act on such a thing would be a disaster.
Business would suffer. Jobs would be put at risk.
Perhaps, the whole global economy would unravel.
So for now, this was steady work.

And, even though, his voice seemed to be returning a little bit every day,
he harbored little desire to return to the corporate Mosh pit.
That life now seemed to him even more preposterous
than earning his keep wearing a gorilla suit.

For he knew, that like him,

we all longed to breathe free and hit the open road,

to re-invent ourselves,

and to know that

no matter what mask we are forced to wear everyday,

that we are all only a tank of gas,

and a costume change away,

from salvation.

By Chris Chandler and Phillip Rockstroh
Originally released on the album *Posthumously Live* (2000)
and *American Storyteller Vol II (2005)*

The Weasels

When I was barely a teenager, I had dreams of one day being able to hang out with the garage band up the street.
They were called *Pythagoras* – it was the '70s – and the sort of philosophical concept rock was popular amongst adolescents.

Now, I wanna take this opportunity to apologize to each and every one of you for my entire generation, for being the ones that brought you
Styx, REO Speedwagon, and Journey.
 It's not my fault.

Now ya gotta keep in mind here that the difference between a thirteen year old and a sixteen year old is great.
So I, as a skinny hyperactive thirteen year old had to have a reason to hang out in the basement with the cool kids of Pythagoras
(or as we said in Stone Mountain: – Pie - thug - orus...)

Well, it was around Christmas – and me in my juvenile delinquent wisdom devised a plan – I would become their lightman.
I went through the suburbs and stole all the Christmas lights in three upscale subdivisions.
I was sort of a blonde haired juvenile delinquent Grinch
– stealing Christmas so that rock and roll would live for ever
– at least in the basements of Stone Mountain, Georgia.

I proceeded to take those Christmas lights into my high school shop class and built a light show.
Soon every garage band at *Redan High School* could not consider throwing a keg party without first contacting "The Light Man."

As it turned out, fate would soon become destiny.

The bass player for one of the bands I worked with had an older brother in a bona-fide bar band called *The Weasels*.

So it came to pass, that I, at the age of fifteen, made my first fake ID, and got a job with *The Weasels,* and soon another band called *The Satellites,* as well as just about every other barband in the city of Atlanta.

But The Weasels were the greatest – a complete gag band.
The singer and songwriter was called Fishman.
He was my mentor, writing songs like
I had a UFO Baby, and *Born too Late to be a Biblical Hero.*

They were the masters of stage antics – even voted "worst band on the planet Earth" by an Athens, GA newspaper.
They filled an Athens nightclub after that distinction.
There was the time they opened up for the LA punk band *X* (still one of the greatest bands of all time.)
They cooked hamburgers on stage from a Bar-B-Q grill and then served them to the audience during the song *Martin the Burger Boy.*

There was the original *Bowling for Beer* and *The Weasel's Wheel of Fortune.*
 One Easter, the Easter Weasel came and led an Easter egg hunt in a single's bar – it was the early 80's and sex was still fashionable – at least in Atlanta.

Once when there weren't many people in the audience,
 they put together a Nerf Baseball game with members of the audience.
Betsy Driscoll hit a home-run that night.

The best was when they got a huge write-up in the Atlanta paper because they managed to get a job opening for a Detroit Motown review called *The Threshold of Soul.* It was a sell out.
The article basically read:
"Detroit soul band coming to Atlanta – obscure novelty act to open."

The Weasels got up and played an average set to a patient crowd.
But when it was over – they went into the dressing room, changed clothes and came back out on stage playing songs like:
Goin' to a Go Go, and *Sad Sad Day.*
They were *The Threshold of Soul.*
Always were.
There never was a Threshold of Soul.

They had managed to dupe every one.

No one wanted their money back.
Fishman remains my hero.

These mistaken-Identity gags would soon come back to haunt them.

They soon got their biggest gig ever: opening for Alice Cooper
at the Tennessee State fair.

Now this was 1981 (the summer before my senior year of high school.)
Well, you may remember in that same summer, The Rolling Stones were also
touring America – with considerably more media attention than The Weasels.

You may also remember that The Stones were – in their off time – going to
obscure rock bars and booking themselves under assumed names
– such as *The Wanna-Bes* and most often – *The Cock Suckers* – to play for
unsuspecting patrons.

Now I don't know exactly how many times they did this
– but it made big headlines in Atlanta.
At the time the coolest thing you could say was that you had accidentally
caught The Stones in some out-of-the-way bar.

Well, ticket sales at the Tennessee State Fair were not exactly going well.

I guess someone had over estimated the power of Alice Cooper's
last hit in his career – a song called *Clones*.
(Remember that one? – See what I mean?)

Anyway, the gig came out of nowhere by an odd phone call from someone we
never met.
A man never photographed, but soon to be often quoted in the newspaper –
by the name of (I am not making this up!) – *J.C. Go Forth*.

Shortly after The Weasels accepted the gig, a rumor was started by
one J.C. Go Forth that The Rolling Stones were to appear at the
Tennessee State Fair – opening for Alice Cooper – under the name
– you guessed it: The Weasels.

All of the major media picked up on it.

Someone had gone as far as renting motel rooms under the name
"The Rolling Stones."
The local news interviewed caterers bringing food to the rooms of The Stones.

The major commercial radio station played nothing but Rolling Stones
all week. There was a banner front Page headline that read :

"Will the Stones Play the State Fair?"
(I still have a copy of the article.)

Alice Cooper himself was interviewed, saying if Mick did not show up, it
meant he was chicken.

(I have heard Mick Jagger compared to a chicken before but never in that
context.)

The venue was actually moved from the local stadium to a much larger race-
way.
There were vendors hawking Rolling Stones T-shirts.
People were camping out for good seats.

Inside the raceway, backstage, there were five separate mobile homes
each one with magic marker signs "Mick, Keith, Charlie, Bill, Ronnie."
The weasels changed clothes in Fishman's van, which he managed to park
next to Mick's.

Hell, we thought The Rolling Stones would indeed show up!

The place was packed – sold out – over sold – everyone in their Rolling Stones
T- shirts – people held up banners reading "Welcome Rolling Stones".

Uniformed armed Tennessee State Troopers led me to the lightboard.
I have never before or since had so many people in a uniform claiming to be
on my side.

People from the audience yelled up, "Are you The Stones soundman?"

"No, I thought – I am The Weasel's lightman."

Anticipation was at a full fury.
There was no one on stage yet.
The audience's chant was deafening.

"STONES! STONES! STONES! STONES! STONES!"

A lonely DJ walked out on stage. He could barely be heard underneath the roar of the crowd.

"STONES! STONES! STONES! STONES! STONES!"

"Good Evening Ladies and Gentlemen men men men…. Welcome to the Tennessee State fair fair fair…"
The chants subsided, but the silence only amplified the anticipation.
All ears were on the lonely DJ.

"Tonight we have Alice Cooper Cooper Cooper".

The chants resumed.
"STONES! STONES! STONES! STONES! STONES!"

"The Weasels!" (The crowd goes nuts…)

"STONES! STONES! STONES! STONES! STONES!"

"and, (very ominous voice) who knows what else…. "
(Crowd climbing on top of each other in anticipation…)

"Please welcome – The WEASELS !!!!!!!!"

Bottle rockets and Roman candles begin going off, women bearing their breasts…
Out walked a raggle taggle punk gag group from Atlanta.

Well, you must understand that this was a VERY large crowd, whipped up into a very large frenzy.
It took a few minutes for people to figure it all out – some cheered.
Some kept chanting, some looked at each other dumbfoundededly

"That's not the Stones!"

In fact it took about a half a song for the full wave of anger to hit the crowd.

Now The Weasels had carefully selected from their repertoire
a song called *Dead by Christmas*.
They had no idea how prophetic that song would be.

(*Dead by Christmas* is actually a true story about a 10 year old in Arizona
who was paid by his mother to kill his younger brother,
so she wouldn't have to buy Christmas toys for both of them.

This song also has the distinction of having a lead guitar break
follow the first Chorus).

Hot Rod Rake was ready.

So was I.

I was standing in the light booth, headset engaged:
"Follow spot number one on stand by, in frame two, to hit performer three,
down center – on my go..."

Fishman sang,
"Dead by Christmas – bury him after New Year's Day to get him off our tax."

"Follow Spot One – GO."

Hot Rod Rake stepped downstage….

Now the first item to be thrown at the stage was just a piece of ice.
But it was the way in which that sparkling piece of ice entered
the cone of light illuminating Hot Rod Rake.

The ice hit him square in the chest.
It reflected a perfect rainbow of light back to the audience.

At the exact same instant – the whole audience realized simultaneously
– like the hundred and first monkey – that they had all been duped.

Next was cups, cans, bottles, folding chairs – they are lucky there was no gun play – it was Tennessee.

As a lark, the Weasels had put *Street Fighting Man* on their set list – just in case. Fishman pointed to it – Franco F. Woid shook his head no – and The Weasels lived to tell the tale

"What can a poor boy do 'cept to sing for a rock n roll band?"

Alice Cooper played to half a house.

Mick Jagger it turned out – was chicken.

The Weasels actually got a favorable review in the paper
– out of sympathy I am sure.
It read that The Weasels were so good, that they didn't deserve to get booed off stage. How's that for a quote?

They were asked in an interview after the show,
"Have you ever billed yourselves as the Rolling Stones before?"

Fishman replied, "No, but it would help record sales."

As for me… I continued to work lights for The Weasels for several years.

I also worked for that other band I mentioned – the Satellites
– for about 5 years all told – but I quit the group
– three weeks before they got their record deal, changed their name to *The Georgia Satellites*, had a number three hit called *Keep Your Hands to Your Self*…

They too eventually broke up...

Me, I'm still on the road.

I visit Fishman from time to time.

Written in Stone Mtn, GA in 1995
Originally released on *American Storyteller Vol IV* (2007)

A Tribute to Gamble Rogers

I had tried forever to get Deborah Fliehive to go out with me.

She was in my history class at (I'm not making this up) DeKalb Community
College.

After months of requests, bids pleas, surveys, appeals, inquisitions,
explorations, and everything short of a begging,
the poor woman finally agreed.

We were to go see the band Pylon at The Moon Shadow Saloon.

The date was set.
Fake Ids were pressed.
Every trick in my nineteen-year-old arsenal was loaded,
cocked and the safety removed.
I was a double barreled pre-meditated mess.

"I know the guys in the band," I told her.

(Well, really I only knew the guy that ran the lights
but I could fake the rest.) I was ready to impress.

I figured once she saw me hangin' with the band,
she'd be all over me, and her perception of
the nerdy history geek at DeKalb Community College,
clad in parachute pants, pre-ripped T Shirt,
and every other accessory the 1983 edition of
the Davidson's Department Store Catalogue had to offer
would be forever shattered.

Its pieces would then be dispersed into the
optimistic back seat of my Toyota Corolla.

Life was lookin' good.

She was leanin' in on me when the bouncer accepted our fake ID's.

But then…

Unfeigned reality crushed me like a falling anvil – and this was no cartoon.
There was no Pylon.
There wasn't even rock and roll.
I had gotten the dates wrong.

Pylon was playing tomorrow night.

Some guy – as I perceived the calendar – who did a Kenny Rodgers cover of
The Gambler was playing.
"Gamble Rogers," it read.
"The Troubadour Emeritus of Oklawaha Country Florida."

On top of that – it was sold out.

As we stood outside on the sidewalk,
I was making fast excuses and riffling through
the local arts weekly known tauntingly, as *Creative Loafing*.

Deborah's impatience was becoming plain.
My ability to improvise was dwindling.

Then suddenly, the black and orange sign
that hung on the large double doors which read
"You must be twenty one or older to enter"
came swinging towards us. A couple walked out.

An ordinary couple, I mean how do I put it?
They seemed very ummm... square...
as in anything they liked – I would not.

It turns out the guy was a doctor, and he had been paged on an emergency
call. The couple offered us their tickets, and we accepted.

"You won't regret it," he told me.

"I already do," I thought.

As we made our way to our seats,
out walked a skinny man with a guitar,
playing like I had never heard a guitar played,
as he just talked to the audience.

Talking to me.

He proceeded to completely captivate
the audience which I had now willingly joined.

He was a great picker – at least I told myself.
(Other than the intro to *Stairway to Heaven* and *Freebird*
I don't think I had ever listened to an acoustic guitar.)

This guy was such a great storyteller,
that I didn't even notice that somewhere in there
he had stopped playing the guitar.

Deborah however noticed.
She was tapping her plastic magenta dancing shoes
to a beat she heard in a crosstown club.

He was telling tales of Narcissa Nonesuch, Still Bill,
and Agamemnon Jones.

I was hooked.
"That's what I want to do." I thought.

I tried to tell that to Deborah.
But she had managed to find her own way home.

I didn't care.

I had discovered what I was looking for.
Only I wasn't really looking.

I tried to meet him afterwards – but it didn't happen.

I did however, go home convinced that what he was doing,
was what I wanted to do with MY life.

I spent the next few years honing my craft,
and eventually wound up on the same label as Gamble Rogers
(although my record on Flying Fish stinks – Gamble's is terrific.)

I finally did meet him backstage at a
Fish Fry and Folk Music concert in rural Texas.
I had told someone what a huge fan I was,
and what an influence he had been on me.

I was introduced – and found myself tongue-tied with nothing to say.
I started shaking his hand and forgot to let go.

It was one of those classic
"finally got to meet one of the real artistic influences of my life situations."

I remember that he listened intently, smiled, made direct eye contact
and seemed to understand what it was I was really communicating
as I babbled incoherently about how wonderful he was.

And he was.

Gamble Rogers died a couple of months later.
He drowned while trying to save the life of another man.

Here's to you.

Written in Chicago in 1993
Previously unreleased

A Toast to the Stage Hands

So this lawyer dies and gets into heaven.
Saint Peter says, "Welcome to Heaven, come on in."

This politician gets to the pearly gates,
and Saint Peter says, "Welcome to Heaven, come on in."

This stagehand gets there, and Saint Peter says,
"The loading dock is around the back."

Ya know the difference between a homeless person and a stagehand?
A laminate.

That's how most of the jokes go…

'Cause ya see…

The stagehand never gets celebrated.
He is too busy setting the stage for the celebration.
In fact, there can be no celebration without him.
Nothing like doing the load-in for your own party.

So I say it's time for a toast to the stagehand…
… the noble profession.
The world's third oldest profession.

The stagehand.

I mean the oldest is the prostitute.
The second is the pimp.
Somebody had to set the stage
for the ultimate in live entertainment.

So…

Here's to you, the stage hand… all of you …

The wrench-slingers, the truss-climbers, the box-pushers and dock-jockeys,
the color girls and best boys, the cookie-cutters,
merch mongers and back-line humpers.
The leggers of decks, the guitar and drum techs.
The tour managers, the projection
booth anglers, and dog and pony wranglers.
The shop stewards and dressing room screwers.

You know why sound men only count to two?
"Check one, two" 'Cause on "three" you have to lift.

What do you call a stage electrician with a hammer?
A thief.

Here's to you and all your quirky rivalries.
May the war between the tweaks and the squints forever rage.

I sometimes think the rivalry was created by
management, knowing that the two would
so often race each other to get their rig up first ,
as we all push towards that moment –
the one we all do this for –

that second when the house lights go to half...
and the hushed silence befalls the crowd…
and then they go out.

THAT!

That is the most important moment in the universe.

For it is in that second
ANYTHING can happen,
(and it usually does.)

If we have done our job, we can sit together beneath the blue lights,
headsets engaged, and listen for the moment,
in which you can actually hear the squeaking of a hinge,
that could only be the opening of the door to wonder.

You know how many stage electricians it takes to screw in a lightbulb?
It's not a lightbulb, it's a lamp.

You know the difference between a stagehand and a pig?
You won't find a pig wandering around a hotel lobby looking for a stagehand.

Without the lights, the show would be… radio.
So tune in my friends – stay tuned – and tune that damn thing.

From usher to producer, diva to downrigger,
performer to intermission lobby bartender,
not a single task more important than the other.

Yes, here's to you…
behind the lights,
behind the set,
behind the marquee,
behind the mask,
behind the scene,

YOU are the scene!

Here's to the finest of the fine print in the program
– the finer the print, the finer the job.

The ushers, the catchers, the shooters, the handlers,
the roach coach poachers, and the ghost lamplighters.
The LD, the SD, the CD, the TD, the SM, the MC,
the ME, the PA, A1, L2, and 3D glasses passers.

Here's to you, show people…
'cos there's no people like show people like no people I know.

Here's to you that put the "U" and the "S"
– the "US" in show business
– by putting the "You" in US.

Written in Baltimore 2010
Originally released on *Matadors* (2012)

Pay No Attention
to that
Corporation
Behind the Flag

The Lousy Parts of Socialism

There I was stuck in a traffic Jam
on the highway to Hell,
honkin' my horn at the devil himself.... shoutin',
"Can't we get a move on?"

We got half of us working a lousy construction job,
tryin' to widen the highway to Hell,
and the other half workin' on
a more fuel-efficient handbasket.

Arguing' with the bank
over which one of us is more alive
– us or them.

But what do the banks know?
They base how alive you are
on what your credit rating is.
Now, the banks have all failed and
people wind up with nothing.

It's like my friend Roger Manning used to say,
"People work hard their whole lives – wind up with nothing.
Me, I ain't got nothing but at least I didn't work hard for it."

In fact, not only are them banks not alive,
they spend all their days and hours trying
to kill anything that might resemble life.

Giving us Service Charges, Late Fees,
ATM Fees, Debit Card Fees,
Over the Limit Fees...

Then ya can't pay all that, and they change your interest rate
from zero to forty percent
and God knows ya can't pay that

– but you try – you're an honest person
– and then what do they do?
They give ya a Bounced Check Fee.

It is no wonder we are in this mess!
We have based our entire economy
on finding folks like me and you
who are broke, and then charging us for it!

They actually look at us in the unemployment line
and circle us like vultures sayin',

"We'll get rich rich rich!"

But what happens when the banks go broke?
Their CEOs make a king's ransom
with their golden parachutes.
(I only wish it was a real parachute made of gold
– Like King Midas jumping out of a 727.)

Them banks are a bunch of
deregulatory Robber Barons,
when they are making money.

But Hell, Robber Baron ain't good enough for them…
At least the Robber Barons of the Gilded Age
– Mellon, Vanderbilt, Rockefeller
– they left us with concert halls, public libraries and museums
– some of the finest buildings ever made.

What do today's Robber Baron's leave us with?
The Sam Walton Junior High Sports Complex in Texarkana, Arkansas?
Put it next to Carnegie Hall – Hell, you can hardly tell the difference.

But when they start losing money,
they change their tune!
They become a bunch of
Commie pinko bastards
giving a handjob to the corpse of Khrushcvev.

But that ain't a hard-on – that's rigor mortis!
We only wind up with
the lousy parts of Socialism.

I don't want to own the banks,

Where's my healthcare?!

They are always sayin' on the news
how Obama is some kinda Socialist.
Really?
I wanna know one thing then?

WHERE'S MY SOCIALISM?!

Why didn't he take over the banks?

Then maybe we could ask them for Service Fees.

We should charge THEM
Late fees, ATM Fees, Debit Card Fees,
Over the Limit Fees...
Bounced Check Fees.
We should be circling them like vultures.

We'd be rich rich rich!

Written in Washington, DC in 2008
Originally released on the album *So, Where Ya Headed*? (2009)

Jello-Wrestling Your Demons

If a ghost can walk through walls,
why doesn't he fall through the floor?

I was thinking about this
when I felt myself being stared at... by the Abyss.

Which made me realize,
I was on the edge of something really big.
I was standing upon a great precipice.
(Which is probably not a good moment to put your best foot forward.)

I like the metaphor of Hell being beneath us.
Sometimes, ya gotta go down there
and wrestle your demons.
Hell, sometimes ya ya gotta go down there
and jello-wrestle your demons!

When you're going through Hell – ya gotta just keep going.
'Cause the world is round, and you'll come out on the other side,
wondering why everyone is speaking in an Australian accent.

Down is the new up.

This is why I think the Republican party had the perfect candidate
in an ultra-rich guy like Mitt Romney.
I hope they find more like him
– a guy whose personal income
outweighs the entire net worth
of all the right wing whackos he's kissing up to
by going down on the likes of Donald Trump.

Down is the new up.

Now, these ultra rich politicians on the right
– in truth – could really care less about any of this
whacko conservative agenda they pretend to embrace.

Eliminating a woman's right to choose....
They don't really care...
but they will stand in front of a shopping mall saying:

"No, that's not far enough – let's ban contraception altogether...
lets even ban embryonic stem-cell research
– Hell – let's legislate that life begins at conception..."
(which would mean I'm not really a Capricorn,
I must be an Aries... but I digress).

The only reason the rich have to be against abortion –
is that poor people having babies assures them a cheap labor pool.
I mean, I'm sure the overseer was pro-life.

But trust me when their daughter Madison
gets knocked up by the pool boy...

So, while we are at it, the ultra-rich
don't really give a rat's rectum about
gay marriage either
– largely because they don't give a rat's rectum
about gay people.

Not only that, the rich don't give a flying firetruck
about the right to bear arms.
In fact, they would rather the poor not have guns.
I mean, without government
(which is what they really want)
the poor are their only real threat to power.
If I were rich I wouldn't want us armed.

But as long poor people are only shooting other poor people,
and as long as as there are more people at the gun show
than at the poetry reading,
the ultra-rich will remain staunch supporters of the NRA.

Nor do they really give a wooden nickel
(an oxymoron by-the-way)
about illegal immigration.

You would think they would be for it
because "those people" work cheap.
However, the truth is,
they can afford to move their factories to poor countries.
They don't need the cheap labor to be here.
They just need it to be somewhere.

Moreover, no self-respecting billionaire
cares about the Church either.
Sure they give money to the Church,
but we all know giving money to the Church
doesn't make you a good person,
any more than buying tickets to the game
makes you a third-baseman.

What the Church offers to the rich is
– people.
The only thing in the world the One Percent does not have
is... people.
Ninety Nine Percent of us to be exact.

In short, as long as there is something resembling a government,
they need a large number of people to support them.
So they will say anything to us to stay in power.
But they don't actually believe what they say.

The truth is:

The rich don't care about social issues
because they don't LIVE in society!

They have their own police force, their own schools, their own hospitals
– soon they will have their own military!

I am not afraid of Iran getting the bomb.
I am afraid of Exxon getting the bomb!

The rich just support whatever they think
the majority of the impotent insolvent will vote for.

This is why they need Tea-Cup Poodles
like Rick Santorum, Michelle Bachman and Sarah Palin
who can shift the limp moral compass of the masses
so they think they are taking the high road.

Walk softly and carry a big carrot
(which is of course attached to a big stick.)
But my friends, that kind of a high road...
...will lead you off a cliff.

I picture the entire staff of Fox news
leading the masses like asses up the high road,
and then dangling the carrot off the edge,
then boasting of all the jobs that are being created down at the mortuary.

But personally, I'll stick to the low roads,
because storytelling is the art of telling truth with lies.

That high road the others claim to be on is simply a lie.
Down here... I don't have to worry about falling off a cliff
– because like I've always said,

"If you think there is a cutting edge – than you ain't on it."

(Which is why I don't think this is that "edgy" of a thought...)

If the rich can cross the lines between right and wrong
like ghosts walk through walls
– maybe it is time they also fell through the floor.
Maybe they will go straight to Hell.

And maybe – just maybe – we will all
come out on the other side.

Written in Oakland 2012
Previously unreleased

9th Ward New Orleans #6

A hundred and fifty years ago,
corporations were granted the same rights as people
under the Constitution.

It is called Corporate Personhood.
I have been against this concept for years.

But alas, after this incident in the Gulf of Mexico
(soon to be known as The Dead Sea,)
I see the error in my ways.

So, I now say,
"If corporations want the rights of citizens...
they should also have the accountability as citizens."

I mean, I know if my negligence caused the death of eleven people
– let alone the destruction of the entire Gulf Coast
I would be......in prison!
So, I say,
"Put the entire payroll of British Petroleum in prison!"

How do you like you Corporate Personhood now?

I envision not just the CEO
going to prison
I wanna see every Executive Officer
GO TO PRISON!
Every V.P. S.V.P. and V.I.P. for that matter...
GO TO PRISON!
Every CFO, every CIO, CISO CPA and C-3PO...
GO TO PRISON!

Make an example of them – just like you make an example
of the guy sitting in prison for smoking dope in his own apartment.
If there is not enough room for the entire payroll of British Petroleum
in the prison system, let the guy who is in there for smoking dope out

to make room for the corporate guys.

I wanna see the writers and the actors in those
B.S. BP ad campaigns
"Beyond petroleum, a greener oil company."
...GO TO PRISON!

I envision whole gas pumps dressed in orange jump-suits
quivering with their little British accents
as a large scary man, stands over them saying, "insert prison joke here."

I wanna see every seller of every British Petroleum...
GO TO PRISON.
I wanna see every user of British Petroleum...
GO TO PRISON.
I wanna see every user of petroleum...
GO TO PRISON.
Hell, I want to...
GO TO PRISON!

As we all watch the BP bank accounts and
the bank accounts of Haliburton and Transatlantic
drained while they are paying the billions... quadrillions in reparations.

Haley Barbour, you can lick my dip-stick!
I say it is time to "Bill Baby Bill!"

I say you should drain your coffers by employing
every idle shrimp boat captain and his crew
in every idle boat in every dock
in every port from Miami to Brownsville
to clean up your mess.

You should spend every dime
hiring every out-of-work oyster fisherman in Pensacola
and unemployed seafood restaurant waiter in New Orleans.
Use the community we have!

I wanna see your shareholders

standing on off-ramps holding buckets with signs that read
"will work to pay locals for their loss."

You knew your oil rig was too big to fail.
That's why it was flying a flag claiming
it was from the Marshall Islands.
The Marshall Islands is just another oil company with a flag.

But since you did choose to fly the flag of the Marshall Islands,
I say it makes you an Illegal Immigrant
and I find myself suddenly agreeing with the State of Arizona
and I believe, "You should be deported."

And a crime like this – perpetrated by a foreigner –
can only be viewed as foreign eco-terrorism.

So, the place you should be deported to is
Guantanamo Bay
where you can sit in your little orange jump-suits
and be water-boarded...
with water...
from the Gulf...

YOU DESTROYED!

Written in New Orleans in May 2010
Previously un-released.

Carnivals #5

In times of great crisis the world turns to great leaders
– Winston Churchill, Franklin Roosevelt
– and what do we get?

Well hang on ladies and gentleman!
This is a visit to Six Flags over Mecca
and the rides in this carnival are very, very dangerous...

She flies through the air with the greatest of ease
The beautiful girl on the flying trapeze

"Ladies and Gentleman! Step right up.
It's a visit to one of those genuine, carnivals of olde.
Complete with cabinet freak shows
and multinational corporate clowns,
and a phony western Sheriff leading a horse opera shooting gallery.

"We've got phony media mad-men hyping the election game-show
like carnival hucksters pitching a rigged game
that was impossible to win.

Leaving us to pick the cheap prize that no one really wanted:
Forrest W. Gump – a tiny stuffed buffoon dressed as a stuttering Wyatt Earp
in a bad Ronald Reagan western – standing on the trophy shelf
to the right of his father, Ronald Reagan and Richard Nixon."

Hey you with the red checkered hat on.
Would you like to see what you've won.
A world of adventure is waiting
For you behind door # 1.

See the Puppet show
– with a return visit from many old favorites from the original cast.
We've got Dick Cheney as Elmer Fudd, Donald Rumsfeld as Yosemite Sam,
and, in his last performance, Jessee Helms as just plain Goofy.

(For tonight's performance,
the role of Clarence Thomas will be played by Al Jolson.)

Colin Powell plays Pluto, Mickey Mouse's viscious guard-dog
who is the only character in all of Disneyland who does not speak.
This show once featured Ronald Reagan as a marionette for big business,
but now the same old guys have their hand
stuck so far up the tight rectal sphincter of Little George
that they can operate him like a handpuppet.

Thrills spills and adventures,
you'll cry you'll scream and you'll laugh.
Take a peak behind the red door
for only a buck and a half..

Ladies and Gentleman! Step right up! It's a shell game!

Which rock is Bin Laden hiding under?

While you stand there mesmerized,
you find your pockets have been picked
and your civil liberties vanish before your very eyes.

All around you, the carnival hucksters cash in with T shirts
(made in sweat-shops in Bangladesh – a Muslim country)
while CNN asks,
"Why do they hate us?"

In fact our whole culture has grown so distorted
it can only be viewed from the fun-house mirror.

HA HA HA HA HA HA

Today, when we see our world in the fun house mirror
it is so distorted the reflection seems normal.

For example: the President has repeatedly declared
that despite his rather unfortunate choice of the word "crusade"
– this is not a war against Islam –

for their extremists have some very good ideas,
such as public flogging.

Yes indeed, it's a house of mirrors.
With all the confidence of a snake oil salesman,
George Bush claims that we were attacked
because we are the beacon of freedom and opportunity
and has nothing to do with our desire to
turn the world into a shopping mall,
and he can make the world safe from these terrorists
by telling us, "Buy more stuff!"

New flag for your SUV? $19.95
New SUV? $40,000!

Looking more patriotic than your neighbors…
…Priceless."

The bright lights make you dizzy,
as the big wheel spins you round.
You can almost smell the heavens,
until the big wheel brings you down

He claims he wants to make America safe from terrorists.
By getting rid of so many civil liberties,
he can fool the terrorists into thinking this is Afghanistan.

And if you really like the fun-house mirrors
– consider this, George –
if you really want to bomb everyone
who funded, trained and armed Osama Bin Laden,
perhaps you should start with your dad.

Would you like to buy a bottle
We swear you will never grow old
Takes lines from your face it'll get you a date
It cures the common cold

Though elected by
the overwhelming indifference of the American people,
recent public opinion polls now shows them
divided between the patriotic and Jingoistic.

15% saying that the ability to find Afghanistan on a globe,
should not be a requirement for the Commander-in-Chief
just so long as we nuke somebody.

23% saying, failure to display a flag that
does not cover the entirety of a house, lawn and at least 2/3 of a sidewalk,
is documentable proof of Islamic militant tendencies,
and is grounds for deportation or internment
(And in truly egregious cases, that person
should be forced to watch a Lee Greenwood concert.)

…and I'm proud to be an American
Where at least I think I'm free
to get six miles per gallon
in My cool Jeep Cherokee

and I will Stand up and Kick your ass
if you're different than me.
There ain't no doubt in one's mind…
… I love my S. U. V.

We Americans now long for
the golden comfort of the familiar
as the carnival continues to expand.
America gets back to Normal – "gGo to Disneyland" the president exclaims.
That will show the terrorists that America is strong,
and its culture superior.

Our mighty strip malls and department stores
homogenize every speck of variety
so that the only sense of innovation we have anymore
is new and different ways to export super sized blandness
to every possible customer in the global theme park.
The Hard Rock Café, Islamabad, Six Flags Over Mecca

and at the food court, we may have to convince Mexicans
just what a Chalupa Supreme really is.

But, hey, Taco Bell is
"The People's Taco" (registered trademark)
but that's nothing compared to:
The Mc Muslim Burger?
A Samosa with Cheese?
Mc Hoof and Mouth Disease?
or K.F.C.I.A.?

Go See Madam Zelda
her crystal is true to the end
She'll tell you about your future
like how much cash you will spend.

It's like a mantra or a sing-along…
…being sung by Disney-like mechanical heads of states,
operated by the all powerful Wall Street Wizards of Oz…

Pay no attention to that corporation behind the flag!

But no matter what they sing:
It always ends with…

"It's a small mind after all."

By Chris Chandler and Anne Feeney
Released on the album *Live from the Wholly Stolen Empire* (2004)
and on *Flying Poetry Circus* (2002)

Twenty-First Century
Skid Row Man

And there I was thinkin' that
the 20th century was never going to leave!

He'd been hangin' round my house – sleepin on my couch,
puttering round my living room in his socks
like Ozzy Osbourne, nothin' to say, burnt-out, still an oil junkie,
re-livin' his past glory – aging chunky trophy-wife,
worthless irritating brats runnin' around,
small dogs soiling the carpet…

But then the 21st century arrived
aboard four airplanes
right into my living room…

All the pundits claimed that we had changed.
But what I want to know is
– how is it that we have changed?

Remember when all the pundits said
we Americans would never go back to our reality show lives
– that the endless imagery of the Twin Towers falling
would make us think reality itself was a good enough show
– and that Survivor would not survive – and there would be an end to shows
like *American Idol*, *Real World*, and *Who Wants to Marry a Republican*?

We have NOT changed!

Sure, before 9-11 the American flags
that had flown tattered on the antennae of gas-guzzlers
had finally blown threadbare. Now new ones are
as ubiquitous as retired generals on the FOX news network.
So called "reality shows" that depict a reality
that I couldn't hallucinate even during my drug days
are more popular than an Ecstasy and Viagra cocktail in a techno dance club.

But, there was that moment that we all keep re-living:
when the 20th century had indeed left the house.
And in that moment, as the door shut behind him,
I believed the phoenix that we all knew would
arise from the ashes of the Twin Towers
might turn out to be a dove.

Then we saw L'il W on the White House lawn
– clearly suffering from mad cowboy disease, spatula in hand,
standin' in front of a George Foreman grill, …
serving up fillet of dove, and dove Mc Nuggets.

And in that moment, I knew the 20th century hadn't left for good
– No, Ozzy Osbourne had just stepped out for a pack of cigarettes
and he was back – in my living room! On a fresh oil jag –

And he plops down on the couch, flips on the latest reality show
– called Survivor: Iraq
– hoping the contestants will not simply vote each other off the battlefield –
and he's shoutin',

"USA! USA! USA!"

as the smoke rises.

I think back to 9-11 and of
the pundits asking for that moment of silence.
Every time I see the bombs falling
– every time I hear those chants of

"USA USA,"

I wish SOMEONE would ask for another moment of silence.

A year of silence.

A millennium of silence!

But no one does…
…And I realize
that what they were really asking for
with their moments of silence was for
ME to be…
…well…
…silent.

And I was…
well, as silent as I could be

As we bombed Afghan mud-huts into the stone age,
and turned a country led by a brutal dictator
into an oil company with a flag –
giving birth to ten thousand more terrorists
with each bomb that falls.

So you see – the 20th is up to his same old tricks…

"We'll prove Iraq has the bomb – if we have to plant it on them ourselves."

Oh, what was it that PT Barnum said,
"There is an American born every minute?"

I envision a new reality show – one much more wholesome –
(perhaps it should be shot in black and white.)
It features George Senior, not Ozzy Osbourne,
puttering around the summer house in Kennebunkport,
like Fred Mac Murray, wearing a cardigan and muttering to himself.
"What to do about those pesky kids: Neal and Jeb and Little George".

We'll call it "My Three Sons".

Barbara, baking cookies in a Martha Stewart apron.
Millie is doing her doodie on rug.
Jeb calls up and asks,
"Daddy, if we introduce democracy into Iraq,
does that mean Florida might be next?"
Then Neal drops by, asking for his allowance, and announces,

that the Supreme Court has just ruled 5-4
that he should be the democratically-elected President of Iraq.

L'lil George comes over for his history lesson. Dad asks,
"Now George – who was the first President of The United States? "
George gets that confused look on his face
– that we've all grown to know and love – so Dad says,
"I'll give you a hint – the picture is on the one dollar bill."
L'il George looks at the one dollar bill and smiles and says,
"Mommy!"

Dad gets the globe off the shelf
and tries to show him the difference between
the Persian Gulf and the Persian Cat.
And George looks at the globe as his father points.
He sees the very place that civilization began
– and something inside him stirs.
Something makes his tiny heart swell – just a little bit.
as he announces, "That's where the bombing begins!"

Sometimes listening to George Bush
is like reading the first chapter of *Genesis* in reverse.
I mean I know he has dyslexia and all…

"And in the end – the world was a shapeless chaotic mass."

"No, No, No, George, it is *In the beginning… the BEGINNING…!*"

Is it any wonder why – in that region –
as civilization was in its infancy
human beings wandering aimlessly through the desert
– that they found their liberation their salvation,
their hope – in a burning…

Bush?

By Chris Chandler and Anne Feeney
Originally released on the album
Live from The Wholly Stolen Empire (2005)

FM Revisited Again

I thought we had left the seventies well behind.
But here I am stuck in another gas line.
I pulled out, and wouldn't ya know,
I rear ended a 1973 cricket green Pinto.

And I felt the seventies grip even tighter,
as that car went up like a disposable lighter.

It blew apart as it did explode,
And an eight track tape... hurled through the air...
crashed through my windshield,
and lodged in my frontal lobe.

The seventies and the present began to merge,
as I heard myself singing these words:

Do a little dance,
Make a little love,
A little muskrat love.
May I have your attention please?
Will the real Slim Shady please stand up?
We're gonna have a problem here..
Lets do the time warp again.
Ooops I did it again,
Wake me up when September ends

An unpopular war drags on.
Gas prices rise and rise.
A cloud of scandal gathers over Washington D.C.

Sound familiar?

We wake up, hungover, on the couch,
trying to decide the difference between
the Gong Show and *Survivor.*

Perhaps we really did sleep through the 80s and 90s.

And who can blame us,
after taking the Quaaludes of
Ronald Reagan, George the First, and Bill Clinton.

At least that's the encrypted message I've been able to decipher,
using my Super-Secret, Decoder Mood Ring,
special limited, Karl Rove edition.

George W. Bush and Karl Rove are as much products of the 1970s
as Herpes Simplex Retrovirus.

Historically, the world will regard the Bush Administration
as the Dacron Polyester of American presidencies:
the *Pet Rock* of the American plutocratic class.

I ain't gonna bump no more with no big fat woman
What you gonna do with all that junk?
All that junk inside your trunk...
She's a brick.... house.
I'm a gonna
get, get, get, get, you drunk,
Get you love drunk off my hump.
Shake shake shake....
My hump, my hump, my hump, my hump, my hump
....shake your booty.
My hump, my hump, my hump, my lovely little lumps.

Even after Nixon was exiled to San Clemente,
and we took up the mantra
"Our long national nightmare is over,"
we Americans remained uneasy.

We were desperately clinging
to the self-deception,
of our being mere bystanders
to the million Vietnamese corpses
that have risen in our dreams,

as hundreds of thousands of Iraqi dead
haunt our sleep tonight.

Rove, Rumsfeld, Cheney.
These ruthless men are all Nixon's progeny.
They all got away free.
In fact, they prospered in the cynical Watergate era,
as they prosper in the
Iraq-had-NO-weapons-of-mass-destruction
-and we-never-thought-they-did era.
They continue to perpetrate their crimes.

But it is we, the American public, who conjured these psychopaths.

We Baby-Boom teenagers
were not the progeny of the Woodstock Nation,
as the authoritarian types of the era had feared.

As a rule, we used drugs
neither to expand our awareness,
nor as an act of social or political rebellion.
Rather they were utilized as
apolitical agents of anesthesia.

They were a supplement to
the sound and fury
of our pinball machine distractions,
and our self-proclaimed-edginess
of the so-called FM radio revolution,

(that was, in reality, the advent of Corporate Rock,)

just as we call ourselves hip and trendy,
by becoming ourselves,
Big Brother's Collaborators
volunteering for corporate spyware such as Facebook.

So ya wanna be a rock and roll star?
Listen now to what I say

Hey now, you're an All Star, get your game on, get played
Hey now you're a Rock Star, get the show on, get paid
The band is just fantastic .
That is really what we think
And Oh, by the way – which one is pink?
I'm comin' up so you better get this party started.

As the years trundled on,
our customized vans with their
shag carpet, chrome-plated chain-link steering wheel
and quadraphonic sound system
would become Mini Vans, with their self ejecting cup holders,
GPS tracking and an XM satellite radio,
playing the same songs we played on our 8 Track.

It was all about our right to the pursuit of numbness.

The United States was transformed from a republic
into shopping malls
devoid of a public square.

An internalized McMansion
has supplanted the towering glory
of our internal Sequoia trees.
Hence, our roots can no longer reach deep down.
Our branches no longer lift towards the sky of possibility,
reducing sequoia forests to toothpicks
in order to pick from our teeth the bits of charred flesh
of those slaughtered in our imperial wars.

Me and you and a dog named Boo
Who let the dogs out who who who who who who who
Burn baby burn! – Disco inferno!

The United States has become a suburban pothead teenager,
who has grown into a self-absorbed,
Starbuck's Latte-slurping,
Prozac popping,
consumer zombie,

who wants to devour
the resources of the entire planet,
the way he devoured the food from his mother's pantry
when he had a bad case of the reefer munchies.

Through the ensuing decades,
we've continued to deceive ourselves
into believing everything from the crimes of Watergate,
to the inane-ness of the *Gong Show*, (the *American Idol* of its time)
had nothing to do with us.

As a consequence, it comes down to this:
we didn't learn a damn thing during the 70s,
therefore, we've condemned ourselves to relive it.

Yes, it is high time
to strike the gong for Karl Rove,
and his pathetic, dancing, feces-flinging, pet monkey act,
that is presently stinking up the stage
of the Gong Show known as
the American political system.

George Bush, "I vote you off the Island."
Dick Cheney, "You're fired."

And next,
we should turn off the TV,
log off the computer,
walk to the closest mirror,
look ourselves in the eye,
and repeat the phrase,

"I am not a crook."

By Chris Chandler and Philip Rockstroh
Originally released on the album *American Storyteller* (2006)
Based on *FM Revisited* (1992)

There Is Something In The Air,
But It Is Not On The Airwaves

Ya know, we HAVE got it together.

There ARE people in the streets

At the very onset of Oil War Two,
there were already more people on the streets protesting
than there were at the height of the Vietnam war.

There is something in the air, but it is not on the airwaves

If there are a half a dozen Jaycees in Cincinnati,
on a street corner waving yellow ribbons,
Fox News acts like it's a Republican Woodstock.

By the time we got to Fallujah we were half a million strong.

But put a million people on the street ,
and they build a fence around you, and call it a protest zone.

We like to look at Vietnam through the soft focus of Hollywood,
which took the blood of war,
and turned it into rose-colored glasses.

We see thousands of beautiful semi-naked twenty somethings
putting daises in the barrels of M16s,
all to the tune of Country Joe McDonald singing

One two three what are we fightin' for?

It makes for spectacular video.
Sometimes I see these images,
and I want to run naked through the streets singing

Why don't we da do it in the road!

But I know better.

When the first American troops went in to Vietnam in 1964,
there was barely a soul on the streets,
yet people were already singing

Blowin' in the Wind,
and *I Ain't Marchin' Anymore.*

These songs were being released on major record labels.
Mega hits would follow.

Today we have more people on the streets,
yet there has not been a single hit song on the radio.

How could this be?

There is something in the air
but it is not on the airwaves.

It's not like Barry McGuire was a deep thinking anti-war intellectual
when he sang *Eve of Destruction.*
No, he was jumping on a bandwagon,
made possible by people in the streets.

Yet right now, there are more people on the streets
than there was then, but you have to think twice
before jumping on that bandwagon
for fear it might be a paddy wagon bound for Guantanamo Bay.

If you speak the truth on national TV,
your show will be dropped,
regardless of the ratings... ask Bill Maher.

A show doesn't need an audience as much as it needs sponsors.
The sixties protesters were brought up in the brand-loyal fifties.
These kids were major consumers of all kinds of goods.
They queued up to buy groovy *Carnaby Street Mod Gear*
and *Wear Your Love Like Heaven Cosmetics.*

Today's protesters?
They don't BUY anything!

They won't shop at GAP.
They boycott Taco Bell.
Hell, they won't even go to Starbucks.

Oh, before the Berlin Wall fell,
we loved to talk about how it was
the Soviet Union would broadcast only the songs of the state.
And we romanticized that is was our radio broadcasts
wafting in from West Berlin that tore down the wall.

Yet now, the cellphone's in the other hand.
There is a new wall running down divided America,
and it is American radio that is being manipulated
by the agenda of the State.
Because the State has become
indistinguishable from the Corporation.
The Corporation needs sponsors
more than it needs an electorate.

But I am warning you,
there is something in the air...

Soon it will be
the people's broadcasts
tweeting in from laptops and cellphones...
wafting in from the Indy Media and *Free Speech TV,*
that tears down the wall.

This time it will not be the Berlin Wall that falls...

It will be Wall Street!

By Chris Chandler and Anne Feeney
From the album *American Storyteller Vol II* (2005)

Embryonic Citizenship

Hey Hey Mr. Rehnquist!
So you prefer the rights of The State
to the rights of Women huh, Mr. Rehnquist?
I know the reason you threw it back to them, now are you hip?
Because you didn't want to answer a raft of questions
regarding Embryonic Citizenship?

Hey Hey Mr. Rehnquist!
So I'm gonna ask you anyway, Mr. Rehnquist
On my tax return do you mind if I file for an Embryonic Dependent?
Is my unborn child entitled to embryonic Social Security benefits?
Do you mind if I collect my retirement benefits nine months early,
Mr. Rehnquist?

Hey Hey Mr. Rehnquist!
We have full fetal rights now, that's for sure.
But if you don't want an abortion, ya ain't gotta have one, sir.
But you've made pregnancy a private matter between a woman,
her doctor, and the state legislature.

Hey Hey Mr. Rehnquist!
(You've got a lot of questions you gotta answer now that we've got this:)
Embryonic Citizenship.
Incipient residence.
Gonna wreak havoc on the next census.

Hey Hey Mr. Rehnquist!
My birthday ain't the day my folks got off ya see.
But if life begins at conception, I wanna know what it is I'm supposed to be.
I used to think I was a Capricorn, now I must be an Aries.

Hey Hey Mr. Rehnquist!
If life begins at conception – if that's what it is you say...
And my drivers license says 20 years and 3 months is my age...
Then I guess you don't mind if I go into a bar and start drinking today?

Hey Hey Mr. Rehnquist!
What happens if an unborn child causes the death of its mother?
Does that child go on trial for murder – or mom slaughter?
But with your decision regarding capital punishment for minors
– wait a second – that would be abortion!
This gets so confusing...

Hey Hey Mr. Rehnquist!
I heard tale of a woman – got up one morning
claimed her unborn child was gone.
She got on the phone – called up embryonic missing persons.
Next thing ya know – there was a picture of her belly
– right there on the back of a milk carton.

Hey Hey Mr. Rehnquist!
(You've got a lot of questions you gotta answer now that we've got this:)
Embryonic Citizenship.
Incipient residence.
Gonna wreak havoc on the next census.

Hey Hey Mr. Rehnquist!
You talk about birth control as though you were holier than thou.
There is a certain irony in that – cause you sure don't
offer us much protection anyhow.
It's obvious you didn't use no birth control when you screwed
the state legislature and said,
"It's your baby now."

Written in San Francisco 1989
Originally released on the album (Cassette)
Stranded Musician Need Gas Out Of Town (1989)
and on *As Seen on No TV* (1992)

Innocence

Some say we lost our innocence,
that we left Eden's palace,
when a young president's skull and brain fragments
were blown into a pink mist in Dallas.

Or when that mist gathered into a nimbus
of blown blood and mud in the rice paddies and jungles of Vietnam...
Or else when it descended in Washington DC.
as a dense fog, gray as Nixon's jowls, in decades of scandals...

Up to that point, the only threat to our innocence,
had been watching Annette Funicello sprout breasts on national television.
Although our pre-pubescent minds were filled with lust,
we really had nothing to fear,
because Annette Funicello's breasts were not that threatening.
They were more like breast-ka-teers.

But still we wait,
for the return of Valium yellow sunshine,
to burn a hole in this fog,
and return our world into a pastel paradise.

But it does not come.

And as we wait,

a sudden storm, man-made and malevolent,
bursts forth from the Oklahoma prairie,
heaving dust skyward, occluding the sun.
And then four airplanes fly from the twisted heavens,
tear into our man-made mountains...

and each time, CNN reports once again,
that this is our loss of innocence.
(but I ask you:)

How many times can our innocence be lost?

I mean, is a prostitute who suffers total amnesia
now declared a virgin?

How can we be innocent?
When we plowed our fertile prairies into furrows,
and planted rows and rows and rows and rows of dead Indians,
then watered them with the sweat of African slaves,
and asked the good Lord above
for the ground to be fruitful and multiply,
by performing a ritualistic, salesman's tapdance.

And the good Lord responded,
and the ground was indeed fruitful, and it did indeed multiply,
blooming forth office parks,
strip malls and subdivisions.

Well, it seems to me:
that the proto-typical American
is Mary Kay accessorized with a Gatlin gun.

Did we innocently steal this land?

Innocently?
Like when I was a kid and I wanted a skateboard,
but my mama would not let me have one.
So I took one anyway,
and she made me return it,
giving me a lecture on mine and yours and theirs?

I grappled with this concept, until one day my mama said,
"Be careful with your little sister."
I thought, "Ah, she's my little sister."
So I took her up the street and
traded her to Kenny Jones for a skateboard.

Is this the way we innocently stole this land?
Like a child steals,

or like a dog will eat from the bowl of another?
Because they are still connected to the oneness,
to the holy oneness of everything.

That is beautiful, but it is a strangely Zen concept
for a property-owning nation.

Is this the way we killed tens of thousands
of "guilty" Iraqi civilians?
(Because a bomb does kill innocently.)

Even a so called "smart bomb"
cannot distinguish innocence from guilt.
A truly smart bomb
would blow the guilty to bits,
but leave one whose character leans to the decent.
(Hey! it'd buy him a round of drinks.)

One who's guilty of let's say – a little too much vanity?
– It'd leave them clad in clothes off the rack from JC Penny's.

A sort of smart-ass bomb -
One more Groucho Marx than John Wayne.

These are the fogs and mysteries of our recent history,
and our history is indeed a mystery.

It is a mystery that requires a great detective.
And the best detectives are not Angela Landsbury,
teaming up with Dick Van Dyke, Andy Griffith,
and whatever down-on-their-luck actor,
who hasn't worked in twenty years, looking for any role they can get
– I don't know –
The Partridge Family Murder Mystery Series!
– where they travel around the country in a psychedelic mini van
solving impossible, implausible crimes in the last five minutes...
the guilty are locked up...
so we can guiltlessly consume whatever products
are advertised after the miraculous denouement.

It is time, my friends...

for us to stop declaring ourselves innocent...

and say,

"I was nowhere near the scene of the crime.
I was watching re-runs of *Law & Order* at the time."

Or, do we continue to declare ourselves innocent?

Proclaiming,

"You're God Damned right I'm innocent.
And I will kill anyone who doubts it.

And I will enter Heaven,

even if I have to climb

the mountain

of corpses

beneath me!"

By Chris Chandler and Philip Rockstroh
Originally published in *Protection from all this Safety* (1996)
and on the album *Convenience Store Troubadours* (1997)
and the album *Flying Poetry Circus* (2001)

The rich don't care
about social issues

They don't LIVE
in Society

They have their
own police force

their own schools,
their own hospitals

soon, they'll
have thier own
military

I'm not afraid of Iran
getting the bomb.
I'm afraid of exxon
getting the bomb

On the Set of a
Cartoon Universe

Cracker Jack Cure

Do you remember what it was we dreamed of,
when we dreamed of Sea Monkeys?

I remember thinking of
the magic worlds that would unfold,
like the pages of
Aquaman and *Nemo from Atlantis,*

as I clipped out the order form
for the miraculous-looking
Sea Monkeys
from the pages of a comic book.

But is that the same thing I wanted
as I emptied entire boxes of
Sugar Smacks and *Apple Jacks*
into a large salad bowl
in search of a prize at the bottom?

I remember filling out the order form for
The Cap'n Crunch Treasure Chest,
and camping out by the mailbox until it arrived.

I'll bet I looked in that mailbox everyday,
and if it wasn't there, I looked in the bushes next to the mailbox,
and even in the drainage pipe that ran beneath the driveway.

After six weeks of this, my father,
(not the kind of man to normally contact a corporation to complain)
finally did so.
They promptly replied that they were simply out of stock
and that the Treasure Chest would arrive soon
– restoring my hope
– hope for a treasure
that never would arrive.

But I did finally get my prize…

I remember where I was.
I was at the Circus
with my very first box of Cracker Jacks.

As I sifted through the layers of caramel popcorn
– searching for that prize,
I was somehow oblivious of the sequined beauties
that flew through the air– flipping somersaults with no nets,
and exotic animals which leapt through rings of fire.

I missed it all.
But I did get my prize...

As I was attaching that temporary tattoo of a butterfly to my arm,
I was again oblivious of the magician,
that released an entire flock of live butterflies
from his vest pocket.

What was it I wanted?
What I wanted was a world where all was possible,

Like the Greeks, who stared out across the horizon,
and dreamed of, and believed in,
a land of Minotaurs and one eyed giants,
and islands of Sirens that existed...
just over there...

Just beyond where you can get to.
Why do our gargoyles come from outer-space today?

We as children thumbed through,
and beyond the pages of
our own cartoon universe,
to a world of black and white ads,
– each containing their own mysteries.

Mysteries of decoder rings, X-Ray Sunglasses,
green glowing stalactites,
and the most mysterious of all…
The Miraculous Sea Monkeys.

I realize, I have not changed one bit…
for I am still searching.

Only these days, I am searching through
the caramelized pages of a catalogue,
boasting of an adult prize,
adornments for our corporate Camelot.

I find that nothing leaves me as fulfilled as I was
when I received that brightly colored package,
with images of Sea Monkeys waving to me as they swam by.

And I ran into the living room,
and I ripped open that package,
and I dumped the contents into a large goldfish bowl
and watched breathlessly...

...as two pathetic brine shrimp larva
made their most un-Sea-Monkey-like decent
to the bottom of that bowl!

But still, I think I must be missing something,
for I am still searching for the prize.

I search through catalogues – catalogues of catalogues.
I log on to catalogues.
I log on to something called i-gotta-have-more.com,
where I sift through mountains of caramelized popcorn,
looking for the prize.

Staring at the monitor, but still missing...

...the Circus.

But all of this is not to say that a prize cannot be found.

For there was the time that I opened a catalogue
and ordered a pair of warm wool socks
– oatmeal khaki, (maybe pinot noir.)

Perhaps those socks contained my prize,
for it was in those socks that I discovered the ability
to sit by the fire... eating a bowl of cereal....
Not looking for a prize,
but instead, gazing out the window
at winter's perfection.

I would love to end this tale right here
by saying, at that moment

an armada of golden space crafts arrived,
piloted by a race of alien Sea Monkeys
bearing the gift of my long-lost
Cap'n Crunch Treasure Chest.

Instead, I find that the miracle is not in the miraculous.

Through all of the searching for the stupendous,
the Lotto tickets, *Who Wants to be a Millionaire?*

All I can say is,
"Thank God, we are not given what we want!"

Instead, what we are given
is each day.

Each day is a prize...   a gift...   hidden amongst junk.

By Chris Chandler and Phillip Rockstroh
Originally released on the album *Posthumously Live* (2000),
Live from The Wholly Stolen Empire (2004),
and *American Storyteller Vol II* (2005)

I Dreamed I Saw St. Augustine
(Florida)

It was somewhere between the beginning of time and…
Well… the end of time.
(A little closer to the end, I think, though I can't really say for sure.)

Ya see, I have been to St. Augustine, Florida.
And I have drunk from the Fountain of Youth. I did.
I stood in line for over an hour, and paid eleven bucks for the experience
(and that was with the Triple A discount.)

The water from the Fountain of Youth was served to me in a disposable cup
by a well-tanned teenager, dressed in a red and gold Conquistador outfit.

I didn't think much of it until later that afternoon.
I was at my friend's place in the suburbs, sitting by his pool.
There was that same kid – the well-tanned teenager – still wearing
his red and gold Conquistador outfit, sunning himself in the water.

He was held buoyant by a life-sized inflatable alligator.
The tail wrapped around one side of him, the mouth around the other.
In its snout was a yellow beer Koozie, maintaining an ice-cold Corona.

This kid seemed to be one of those people who never get off work…
as if he actually enjoyed being employed by the Chamber of Commerce,
as if he had posted his list of hobbies to *Monster dot com*.
It matched him up with a Conquistador suit,
and he recognized this as his true destiny.

"Welcome to St. Augustine," he boasted.
"The oldest city in the U.S.
It was here that Ponce de Leon and I searched for the Fountain of Youth.
I was only 19 years old at the time."

"This guy has taken his character a little too far," I thought.
"Like George Bush thinking he really was elected."

"Most people think the Fountain of Youth to be just some foolish Indian myth."

"I don't," I thought.

"Why else would they buy all those ads
for Minoxydil, Viagra, and silicone breast implants?"

(As for me, I keep my Viagra right to my Prozac,
and, ya know,
if either one of them worked, I wouldn't need the other.)

"There must have been some language barrier because the Calusa Indians
weren't talking about a Fountain of Youth that could
melt away cellulite or prevent gingivitis.
They were talking about the youth of the species not the individual.

"It is why, when the Spanish came here, (in search of decent Indian food,
and most importantly gold, and fresh slaves), all the free black sailors that
came over with them started putting two and two together.

"Hostile Indians who knew the terrain better than they did, did not make such
good slaves.
The free black sailors were afraid they might become the slaves the Spanish
were in search of. They built a fort for their own protection."

Yes, the first American slaves were not black.
The first blacks to settle in America were not slaves.

This was well before Plymouth Rock landed on the Indians.
Mention that the next time you meet some Boston blue blood,
boasting of how long ago their ancestors on the Mayflower landed here.

"There seems to be something in the water here,"
he said, leisurely paddling across the swimming pool.

"Those African Slaves I mentioned before knew this too.
They adopted Christian stories about crossing the River of Eternal Life.
(Or at least crossing the rivers between slave territories into free ones.)

And remember, for a couple of hundred years,
slaves went south to find freedom.

It is kind of ironic that the mythology of their captors,
helped the slaves to escape the…
well, the mythology of their captors.

"The Seminole took these former slaves in, gave them room and board,
gave them jobs in their casinos.
The Indian cultures and the African cultures mixed.
Together they invented menthol cigarettes.

"Let me tell you, when Col. Sanders – settling just north of here –
heard about free blacks living in their own community,
he tried to put a stop to it, by hiring Andrew Jackson.

But Col. Sanders' faithful family retainers
teamed up with the Florida State Seminole.
Andrew Jackson surrendered, while slinking back to Washington, D.C.,
to declare victory and become president.

(It's not the only time a defeat in Florida
has led to becoming President – but that is a different story.)

"As for the Seminole, they remain unconquered to this day.
Think about that the next time you go down to Hollywood, Florida,
and feed a picture of Andrew Jackson into a slot machine.
Perhaps the Casinos are the Indians' way of paying white people back for
bringing them the Forty Ouncer."

(I wondered why he didn't tell us all this back at that tourist trap.)

"And I won't bore you," he continued.

"With all the history about the first slaves to be freed by the emancipation
Proclamation – or the first big race riot that eventually led to the end of
segregation all happening right here –
I'll just tell you that it happened… and that in the end,
a man named Martin Luther had a dream that came true.

"That's not to say he was the only one to have this dream,
nor that the present is particularly auspicious.
In fact, today many of the descendants of those former slaves are now work-
ing minimum wage jobs, using the water from the Fountain of Youth
to water the emerald lawns of the Radison, Ponce de Leon Golf and
Conference Center."

It's a glass half empty, half full question.
To which, I say, "Get a smaller glass."

There are millions of problems in this world,
a million of them right here, right now.
But that means there are a million answers,
A million voices and a million dreams.
And every dream comes true.
It's just all in the way you interpret it.

Ponce de Leon, too had a dream, he just didn't interpret it the right way.
His quest in the wrong pursuit, wound up getting him killed,
about a hundred miles south of St. Augustine.

And last night, a hundred miles south of St. Augustine,
in a place now known as Cape Canaveral… the roosters said it best.

They began crowing, as roosters do
– but the thing is – the dawn was not yet upon us.
Yet, the whole horizon bloomed at once.
A misty blue light filled our lungs
as the horizon hurled yellow rage across the water's edge.

Thousands of miles an hour, a blue-grey ribbon
suddenly streaked toward the open arms of heaven.

The air rumbled.

Canada Geese honked across the water, befuddled.
Then a long trail of God's own cigar smoke was all that remained.

It seems the Hubble Telescope was again in need of repair.

Our pictures of the universe had become blurry.
The space shuttle was making a house call this morning.
Three astronauts with a bottle of Windex
had been deployed to clean her mirrors.

The infinite is smaller somehow.
Yes, I said. Get a smaller glass.

From up there, when ya look down on it,
Florida might look like the a giant limp tallywacker
hanging flaccid from that beast now known as The United States.

But if ya think about it, from that drooping Johnson,
mankind ejaculates into the cosmos
– shooting the seeds of the Fountain of Youth
to swim the heavens in search of eternal creation.

We have walked on the moon.
Satellites do probe the galaxies.
There is a Fountain of Youth.

(Which has nothing to do with
Monoxadil, Viagra or silicone breast implants.)

And as I thought about that...
(the Fountain of Youth, not the silicone breasts)

I found myself drifting back into consciousness...
held buoyant by a life-sized inflatable alligator...
in a swimming pool...
in St. Augustine, Florida...

My Corona no longer ice cold...
wondering...
how do I interpret this dream?

Written in Titusville, FL 2002
Read aboard the Space Shuttle - somewhere in outer space in 2002
Originally released on *Live From the Wholly Stollen Empire* (2004)
and *American Storyteller Vol I* (2005)

Yesterday Left Early

History repeats itself.
History repeats itself.
His story repeats itself.
History repeats itself so often it's begun to stutter.

I know this because I met History one time.
It was at a party.
History was hanging out in the kitchen,
talkin' to The Past.
They were talking about Yesterday.
Well, until Yesterday showed up, late of course.

Yesterday said to History,
"You've been saying some awful things about me behind my back.
You don't know, it wasn't like that. You had to be there."

The Past just said, " I am there."

Meanwhile, in the living room,
The Future was hanging out
with his fast-talking friend, Hope.

(You know those guys, they're always the life of the party,
'cause they'll tell people exactly what they want to hear.)

The Present was busy fretting about,
making sure that everyone wiped their feet and tried the egg salad.
She was worried that The Future
might find out she had been sneaking into motel rooms
with The Past.

She was afraid that Time would tell.

Ya know, she once had a brief fling with Hope,
but Hope left the next morning
and didn't even leave his phone number.

The party started to go weird about the time
The Past's ex-wife Memory showed up.
She always brings her lawyer, Regret.
Ya know, from the law firm, Regret, Recrimination, and Denial.

Memory and Regret were arguing with The Past
over custody of their child, Shame.

But, this is not what worried The Present.
She was afraid that people might find out she had
also slept with Regret.
Shortly after she lost Hope.

The Present frequently reduces herself
to just a one-night stand.

Now the party started to break up
about the time The Truth arrived.
You know that guy, he doesn't get out too often.

People started whispering amongst themselves,
"Don't tell The Truth about that after-hours club,
I can never be myself when that guy's around."

Time waited on no one.
The Past got left behind, (caught a ride with Regret.)
As for me, I tried to seduce Lady Luck...
....but you know how that goes...
Yesterday left early.
Tomorrow never came.
Leaving only Truth and History.

And we all know that Truth and History
have never been compatible.

By Chris Chandler and Philip Rockstroh
Originally released on the album *Generica* (1995) and published in
Protection From All this Safety (1996) and the album *Hell Toupee* (1999)

Infinity

Magellan proved Copernicus right by circumnavigating the globe.

Someday, someone is going to prove Einstein was right.
But to do it, we'll have to learn a lot about...
....infinity.

Ya see, Einstein maintained that the universe is round.
He said that every straight line in the universe
eventually intersects itself.

Think about that! The implications are staggering…

It would logically follow that Bill O'Reilly and Sean Hannity
will eventually admit that they are secretly attracted to each other.
That they'll move to Canada… and finally admit
that they've always been… Episcopalians.

Did you know that there are computers
that do nothing all day but try to count to infinity?
I read about it in the paper.
But now, computers count in base two – we count in base ten –
because we have ten fingers.

The Mayans – they counted in base twenty
– because they wore no shoes. (Really.)

As for me, I learned to count from *Sesame Street*.

But, I was thinking…
since The Count on *Sesame Street* only has four fingers
– shouldn't he be counting in base eight?
It left me confused.
So, I learned to count in base eleven
– because I had my hands in my pockets.

In the end, there are ten types of people in the world
– those who know binary and those who don't.

Anyway, the way I see it – if the universe is round,
then infinity is just one digit shy of nothing.
The Bible had a little run-in with infinity that seems to confirm this notion.
Weren't the architects working on the tower of Babel
trying to reach the infinite?
Shouldn't the subcontractors have realized the problem with this project?

Ya get too close to infinity and poof! – you're back to zero.

Ya get too close to Heaven – and ¡poof!
You find yourself speaking Spanish in a Chi Chi's in Dubuque, Iowa,
trying to order *Pollo Guadalajara* ,
and having a teenager in a polyester uniform asking
"¿ya want that with beef or chicken?"

(I went for years thinking *Taco Bell* was the Mexican phone company.)

So one day, one of these computers counting to infinity
is going to spit out that the next number in succession is zero?

It's only a matter of time…
Which will prove that infinity is just one digit less than zero?

So I can tell the bank –
"Hey! I am not four-hundred-seventy-eight dollars overdrawn
– I have nearly five hundred bucks more than infinity"-

Ok, you might not be buying it yet, but I convinced
a half-dozen accountants at Goldman Sachs.
As well as the bank officer who is going to approve my loan for a new Cadillac.

Yes friends,
now I can simply back my way into the two car garage of Heaven.
Only once I get there, I find that
Satan has his SUV parked on the other side.
It's a Ford Explorer with Firestone tires and a bumpersticker that reads,

"This Machine Kills Fascists."

Anyway – the point I am trying to make here is
that if I sit around and count my blessings
– and my blessings are infinite –
and you – by reading this book – give me one more –
will I suddenly discover that I have none?

Seems we are always trying to reach perfection
– like infinity.

Throughout human history
– some new invention comes along that changes us for ever:
the wheel, the printing press, the Lay-Z Boy.

Civilization is changed until we have only vague stories of the past.
"Grandpa – tell me what it was like before Iraq became the 53rd state?"

Civilizations do expand, or they get expanded upon
– It's Manifest Destiny.
But one man's Destiny is another man's Chapter Eleven.
(Or chapter three in base two.)

But the point I am trying to make here is:
the world is round, and

THIS IS NOT A RACE!

And if it were a race, well...
whoever is in first place is slightly behind the guy in last.

And if we could see that,
maybe we would see that the kingdom of Heaven
is indeed spread out before us.

And, if we don't see it – there will be no Heaven – for there will be no here.
Forever.

Written in Victoria, BC in 2004
Originally released on the album *American Storyteller Vol I* (2005)

Dental History

A cloud's shadow passes over the ground.
An earthworm churns the moist soil.
A new generation of day lilies open skyward.
Your lover's touch caresses the nape of your neck
as ancient cities evaporate....

and you arrive at your dental appointment.

Stone monuments melt like hot butter.
Our bodies are digested by God.
Our histories dissolve like a lump of sugar on the tongue.

Death is like a kid in a candy store.
Life is an eternal dental appointment.

Much waiting in torment,
while flipping through back issues of *Life*
waiting on the inevitable bad news...
which will surely be followed by much pain.

The dilemma – do you take the pain and experience life
or do you take the painkiller and sleep through life?

An enormous cavity in your right rear molar has created the effect
of a black hole sucking all life near you into a time warp.
You recline in the dental chair
as time moves backward in your mouth...

Past human history... you spiral backward...
past the inception of the Earth, planets, and stars...
back to the moment of the Big Bang...

Existence disappears into oblivion,
and you don't notice any difference in your social life.

You are in perfect harmony with the entirety of Nothingness.
You've exceeded even the most depressing predictions of your
parents, teachers, and guidance counselors.
Not only did you turn out to be nothing –
but you rendered the whole of the universe that way!

You are the toast of the town, the king of the world.
Clutching the golden statuette
you thank all of those who never believed in you.
Then, humbly give thanks
to a silent, indifferent God
for bestowing nothing extraordinary upon you
and endowing you with just the right lack of purpose
that led you to this shining moment.

Even more than God,
you wish to thank those between-meal snacks
and the entire galaxy of events that combine
to produce tooth-decay, without which,
this grand and glorious achievement would not have been possible.

A bright light blooms before you...
A resplendent being, in gleaming white appears...
She is beautiful, an angelic host.
Her perfect, pearly white smile is just... just... a little too close.

The radiant spirit is... is... wearing latex gloves!

THAT'S NO ANGEL! It is the dentist!

The gas is wearing off!
The tooth containing the cavity of eternal nothingness
has been pulled from your glum, pink gum-line.

You're ruined.
You're forced to return to obscurity.
Obscurity… Like my childhood home which was destroyed
and ugly condos now stand in its place.

If the world could collectively speak, it surely would say:
"It's dinner time,"
and its memoirs would read like a menu....
So I'm having Steak tonight. I'll take it blackened,
and pass the Tobacco.
Don't ask for whom the dinner bell tolls...

So when my time comes I will shout,

"Let the Blue Plate Special shine its ever-loving light on me!"

Even though I was born into this hungry place,
I will resist the temptation of trying to devour the world
like fast food ninety-nine cent value meals....

Instead I will savor life's deathless flavor
– insignificant or not.

By Chris Chandler and Philip Rockstroh
Originally released on the album *Hell Toupee* (1999)

Piloting Paper Airplanes

I stared at a blank page
inside of a new notebook,
dreaming of the worlds that could unfold from its pages.
But the blank page just stared back at me.

So, I ripped it from the notebook,
and folded it into a paper airplane,
and sailed it out the window
of my fourth story apartment building.

I piloted that paper airplane
past power-lines and traffic lights,
and automobile radio antennae,
before I landed it next to a parking meter on a city sidewalk,
and was arrested for littering.

While in prison I accepted a temporary tattoo
that read "Youth."

In my youth,
I remember, my older brother playing with *Match Box Cars*
on the livingroom floor,
making up stories
about the places the people in the cars would go to…
But I was the kid brother.
I could not join him.

Then I remembered.
My brother had borrowed my allowance from me.
(Stolen it really, but we won't go into that,)

In short, he owed me money.
So I made a deal, that I would forgive the debt
if he would just give me that *Match Box Car*.
He did so.

I found myself alone,
with a brand new automobile,
lonely as I ever was.

It was not the car I wanted.

It was the imagination.

That is when I learned,
that just because it is makebelieve,
does not mean I don't believe it….

And more importantly,

just because I believe it,
doesn't mean it's true.

I mean, what is true?

To me, facts are clearly useless,
unless used in a metaphor.

Painting with broad strokes like this,
may cover a large canvas,
but you can't see the picture
unless you are standing on Mars.

And when standing on Mars,
everyone is dreaming
of the rocket and the stars.

And when sailing in a rocket through the stars,
all one dreams of is solid ground.

Perhaps it is good,
that we all want what we can't have.

Because if we had everything we wanted,
what would we dream of?

So go ahead…
Dream of being up there,
in a rocket in the stars.

From up there,
you realize that PT Barnum was wrong.

The greatest show on Earth...
is life.

If you don't like it, you should find better seats.

Once you're in,
it ain't general admission.

So make friends with the usher,
and don't be afraid to crash the gates on the more expensive seats.

To do that, you're gonna need a ladder.
And don't be afraid when you get up there.

Because the harder you fall…
… the higher you bounce.

Which is why I always say,
"I'm so cynical I am optimistic."

What I am trying to say is…
life is sweet…
unless you don't want it to be.

And as any good southerner
who has ever ordered iced tea knows...
for that,
you have to make a special request.

Written in Oakland 2010
Originally released on *Matadors* (2011)

"Let My People Grow!"

I used to never eat meat.
I wouldn't eat anything
that had fallen to the butchers knife.
I was a moral vegetarian,
until I had a vision
that convinced me of
the moral superiority of plant life.

Late one night I stuffed myself
with a broccoli soufflé.
I fell asleep and had a dream,
that still haunts me to this day.

In my bed the nightmare thrashed,
my refrigerator door flew open,
and out of the lettuce drawer
rose the Ghost of Broccoli Past.

He drug me from my bed.
He was angry and emphatic.
He led me to the kitchen,
showed me the executioner's block
of my *Vego-matic.*

He said,
"Look at these terrible atrocities
that you have made."
He pointed out the splattered pulp on the counter
and the flayed skin on the blade.

He said, "This is cruel,
this is horrible.
this is positively
invegitable."

He drug me to the farmer's field,
where the horrible truth was revealed.
He showed me a sight
that all you callous vegetarians should know:
all the innocent vegetables
awaiting execution, lined up on death row.

There were mother radishes
warning their young not to stray too far,
because of the tragic fate that befalls young radishes
who wind up on the salad bar.

There were carrots confined
to the dungeons of the ground
– never allowed to see the sunlight –
and unspeakable medical experiments
being performed on cherry tomatoes,
so they can be consumed in one cruel bite.

All the vegetables shouted out in fear,
as I heard the sound of an engine drawing near.
I tried to run, but could get no farther,
before I was whipped up into a soufflé
beneath the blades of a *John Deere Harvester*.

I wound up in Heaven,
and for my vegetarian sins I fell to my knees.
I begged God himself for mercy,
but he would quarter none of my pitiful pleas.

Because God turned out to be
an omnipotent zucchini.

He changed his mind
and didn't want men feed'n
on any of the life he had meant
for the Garden of Eden.

According to God's new official *Dietary Gospel*
the only thing that we can eat
is that which is man made
and completely artificial.

And so the word came down from up high,
to eat plenty of *Ring-Dings* and *Ho-Hos*,
and wash them all down
with a grape *Nehi*.

So mothers and fathers, tell your children,
if they want to get through the pearly gates,
"Eat plenty of Twinkies
and leave your vegetables on your plates."

To this day people think I am crazy,
for going to the supermarket
and talking to the produce all day.

Compared to most people,
vegetables
have more profound things
to say.

By Chris Chandler and Philip Rockstroh
Originally released on the album (cassette) *Neo-Folk Guitar* (1988)
and published in *Protection from All This Safety* (1996)

Food Not Bombs

Failure

Yes, I know for sure I am a failure.

I remember back in elementary school,
I never wanted to be alone.
So, I'd go play tag with the kids after school,
they all decided I was "it"
then they'd all go home.

Yes, I know for sure I am a failure.

They say every dog must have its day,
on this my curiosity grew,
then they sent me down to the vet to have me neutered,
just to prove it was true.

Yes, I know for sure I am a failure.

The only women who know I exist
are my Mom, and maybe my sister.
And the only ones that will speak to me, are the ones that say
"Hey, mister - you want fries with that?"

Yes, I know for sure I am a failure.

I never even had a woman come over to the house before,
but I once got one to knock at the door.
I answered the door,
I pulled it off its hinges.
But it was just another Jehovah's Witness.
(I asked her in - she turned me down.)

Yes, I know for sure I am a failure.

I failed at everything I tried,
(and I tried a lot.)

I tried to hang myself -
but I was never any good at tying knots.

Did ya know, I competed on *Star Search* one time?
I did...
and I won!

Yes, I know for sure I am a failure.

The Post Office refused to hang up a picture of my face.
My social worker told me I was a hopeless case.
I tried to sell my soul,
but the only customer I got ran a credit check first,
and it was denied.
Suicide prevention said I was over-qualified.

Yes, I know for sure I am a failure.

The army turned me down,
they said I was out of control.
The Rainbow Family said that
my world view wasn't whole.

The Deadheads told me to get a job.

Mother Teresa, she refused to treat me.
Gandhi, he began to beat me!

Alcoholics Anonymous wouldn't give me a cup of coffee.
They said, "Take a drink man, you need it.
Oh, and here's the keys to your car."

Yes, I know for sure I am a failure!

Written in Harvard Square Boston 1989
Originally released on the album (cassette) *In the Road* (1990)

Breakfast Serial Killers

Down in Australia, the ozone layer has gotten so bad
that not only do people accept it
– they are finding ways to cash in on it.

There are beer ads that say:

"Well the world is coming to an end,
but wouldn't you want to die with a Fosters® in your hand?"

Personally, I'm sick of all these visions of the apocalypse,
that have become as plentiful as breakfast cereals
on the aisles of the supermarket of the next millennium.

I'm waiting for ads like:
"The hour is growing late: the Post AlphaBits® spell D-O-O-M."

"The forces of destruction have been eating their Wheaties®,
while the Rice Krispies® of righteousness' grow cold and soggy.

"Perhaps this is the way the world ends:
Not with a whimper or a bang, but with a Snap, Crackle, and a Pop."

The world's goin' to hell and we know it.
Why not make a show of it.
Buy your tickets for the end of the world,
From the breakfast serial killers

The Lucky Charms® leprechaun
is an evil pagan imp if ever I've seen one...

The Trix® rabbit,
(an obvious Marxist terrorist)
is seeking the redistribution of resources from our children,
to subvert 3rd world rodents like himself...

While the Fruit Loops®
bird is a homosexual, drug addict...

The Sugar Smacks® Sugar Bear®
is an androgynous pedophile
looking to lure our children into his cave of perversions
by offering them sugar-coated smack...

Count Chocula®
is an aging goth kid, and after twenty years
he's still painting his fingernails black and secretly hopes
Marilyn Manson® never gets as big as Bauhaus®...

The Cocoa Puffs®
coo-coo bird belongs in a straitjacket.
His bird-droppings have tested positive for cocoa...

The Quaker Oats® guy
is a charismatic cult leader,
leading a band of oddly-dressed,
wig-wearing, mason-like family, Tea-Party
religious fanatic breakfast Serial killers...

The world's goin' to hell and we know it
Why not make a show of it?
Buy your tickets for the end of the world
From the breakfast serial killers

There's mutiny from stern to bow on the Cap'n Crunch® Ship of State.
It's all enough to make you want to head for the beer aisle.
Just say it, say it with me:

Head for the Beer Aisle!
Head for the Beer Aisle!
Head for the Beer Aisle!

Ahhhhh Beer Aisle...
An isle...
like an island of refuge...
an oasis in the dry cereal wasteland...

But there is trouble brewing in six-pack paradise.
The Four Clydesdales of the Apocalypse
ride the random-breathalyzer highways.

A prophet of marketing says to me:

"The end of the world is testing well indeed
And we need nothing less than a major market share of extinction"

Look at the latest numbers.
The Apocalypse is trafficking well in front of the Elysian Fields,
the Rapture, Nirvana, Kroger®, Star Market®, Ralph's®,
the second coming, Piggly Wiggly®

The devil has 100% brand name recognition
among every demographic group....
...all except for one small survey set.

Key groups... Who go to folk festivals,
and listen to NPR,
and find it too all too... too...

Negative...

They like the end of world angle...
Except for one thing...

The ending.

They want a more upbeat Apocalypse!

Something that tells them like Tony the Tiger® does:
that it's all going to be GRRRRRRRRREAT!!!!®

They want a cute, warm-fuzzy product tie in:
a kind of tickle me Anti-Christ Doll®...
or Beelzebub Beanie Babies®.

This is important business here.

This is going to be big.

Bigger than Mardi Gras.
Bigger than the Super Bowl.
Bigger than the Labor Day White Sale.

It's the end of the world, by God –
and if we don't get full sponsorship we are

D-O-O-M-E-D!

GR-R-REAT! **FOR KIDS
(of all ages)**
CHILLED JUICE
SUGAR FROSTED FLAKES
ONE SLICE OF TOAST
WITH JELLY
HOT CHOCOLATE OR MILK
50c

By Chris Chandler and Philip Rockstroh
Originally published in *Protection from All this Safety* (1996)
and on the album *Convenience Store Troubadours* (1998)

Let There Be Prozac

In the beginning
the Earth was without form.
A shapeless chaotic mass,
and darkness was on the face of the deep,
and God said,

Let there be Prozac®.

Ok, it was in the middle of last Wednesday,
and the darkness came across my agitated brain.
And the chaos was strewn across my living room.

And the Lord of everyday insanity...
(and by Lord, I mean a power greater than myself,
which means having to have a job,
and never exhibiting
too much joy or sorrow in public places...)
That Lord of everyday insanity said,

"Let There be Prozac®."

And there was Prozac®,

and it was good.

And so it came to pass that I too cleaned my apartment.
And it blossomed into Eden.

And the corporate trees bloomed abundant with pharmaceutical fruit.
And it too was good.

All grief had been rectified,
not to mention all common household stains and odors had been eliminated.
And all glasses that were removed from the dishwasher
were now virtually spotless.

And in this new land,
all dinner conversation was light and witty,
and non-confrontational,
and no one cared when seating arrangements
involved dining next to the serpent.

For the serpent too is well-medicated,
and a flunky being paid in stock options
by a startup company called
treeofknowledge.com

Satan now sinks before my medicine chest,
and the sign above the gates of Hell reads,
Abandon your medication.

It is the damned that are happily-medicated.

Eternal damnation is not so bad
if you are medicated into the
right state of mind.
(Ask anyone who works ten hours a day
and commutes two hours each way.)

A well-medicated Satan, no longer sows discord
in the *Corporation of Eden*
for he knows a more loving and patient god when he sees one.

God too is medicated.
(Though side effects may include dry mouth,
blurred vision and divine wrath.)

Satan no longer slithers away
humiliated by a second banishing.
For Hell is better than Club Med.

The River Styx® is now brimming with jet skis and recreational boating.
It has a marina with slot machines, and riverboat gambling.
Hell now has casual Fridays and time sharing damnation!

Why does my heart not feel it?

it is not swept clean by this rising serotonin tide.

Why do I wish to take to my bed,
and pull the sheets over my head,
despite all these rumors of impending paradise?

For I do not want to live in Teletubby Land!

I do not wish to dwell in the house
of some creepy infantile totalitarian paradise,
that looks like the contents of
baby Adolph Hitler's acid trip!

All of my dreams are not inexorably
intertwined with the things I buy.

In this bloated bacchanal
of self-satisfaction and greed,
who speaks for the forsaken,
as soil and water evaporates
like the contents of a crack pipe?

Who would see it but the depressed?

And what happens when the depressed
are all jacked up with pharmaceutical cure-alls,
living in a world where all is well.

What happened to the voice that expounds,
Perhaps there can be another way?

You see,
if I could just find a thrift store suit that would never fray.
Or a lime green Gremlin, that would never mechanically falter…
A shotgun shack that would not splinter or crumble.
Then that would be enough.

But finding that not possible,
all I wish to find,
is a durable heart.

And if this heart could swell with gratitude
for these small necessities,
then I would surely find
Heaven's flower blooming in my backyard.

And I would don my humility hat and my gratitude shoes,
and leave the house at a beatific dawn.
And if I should see your oceanic heart,
and sandcastle promises of eternal devotions,
then that would be enough.

And if we were to detour through the park,
and be greeted by ten thousand shades of April's green,
each longing for singular attention.
That would be enough.

Or if we simply happened
upon a single tenacious weed,
sprouting from an unkempt gutter,
that too would be enough.

To see it standing,
defiant,
singular,
rising its head in the chaotic world,
not needing to be watered with Prozac®,

then that would surely be enough.

By Chris Chandler and Philip Rockstroh
Originally Released on the album *Flying Poetry Circus* (2005)

The Grasshopper Steps Up
to the Microphone

I swear I'm not crazy.

I was just out raking leaves when it happened.
I heard this cricket chirp,

"Time is short now, time is short now."

I looked around and thought,

"Yea, time is short...
I've gotta finish raking these leaves.
Look, my neighbors already had their leaves
packed in pristine plastic bags and lined up neatly on the sidewalk.
I gotta be just like 'em.
I gotta finish raking these leaves!"

I began raking more quickly then before,
but as soon as I did,
a brilliant red-yellow leaf floated by and said,

"That's not what he means, man.
Just let go.
Drop into the wind and see where you're blown and buffeted."

"I'm hearing things," I thought.
"I've got to finish raking these leaves."

An angry chorus of angry leaves answered back,

"Don't you dare!
Just listen today, just listen to our symphony of decay."

So I sat on the ground listening to their aria of rot.

I will tell you what they said...

(Though you must understand
that you can never do justice to an opera
by only describing the plot.)

The grasshopper steps up to the microphone.
The ant doesn't listen, he stays at home,
punches the clock, never rosins his bow,
or listen to the grasshopper dosey dosey doe.

"This is our big death scene," they sang.
"You don't put that dead swan from *Swan Lake* in a body bag do you?"

Then I heard the wind perform her number.
She had the raspy voice of a world-weary blues singer,
who had been everywhere, but had never settled anywhere for long.
She sang with such honest suffering, that I too wept out loud.
Her lonesome, sorrowful voice startled the neighborhood leaf blowers,
who admonished me to get back to work.

"This must stop," they demanded. "Get back to work."

I looked around at my unfinished lawn.
I looked to the neighbors who already had their bags
packed up neatly in the corner,
I began to rake once again.
But as soon as I did an acorn thumped me on the crown of my head.

He said, "Forget those pikers.
Why one dream of freedom is worth ten million acts of useless drudgery.

"Don't you see what their angle is?
It's like when your boss walks in the office,
and there is nothing to do,
but yet you find yourself pretending to look busy
doing useless things.
That's what they want.

"They are afraid of what autumn would be like
without the constant sound of.... of...

Pmmwhaahhaawhaaahhhaawhaaaa...

leaf blowers!"

The wind, and leaves, and the sky itself chimed in,

"Forsake the rake!
Blow off the leaf blowers!
Bag the damn bag themselves!"

The grasshopper steps up to the microphone.
The ant doesn't listen, he stays at home,
punches the clock, never rosins his bow,
or listen to the grasshopper dosey dosey doe.

And then... the wind turned cold.

I saw standing before me, in the dimming light of dusk
– the Grim Reaper, himself.

(Now, his appearance was not as I expected it to be.
I mean he was not dressed in a black shroud, or carrying a scythe,
or in any other way dressed as an art student.

No, he was wearing tan khakis, and had a Seattle Mariners
baseball cap perched uncomfortably on his head.
He looked more over-worked than evil,
like my boss trying to look like he was enjoying the company picnic.)

I guess one reason the Grim Reaper looks so, well... grim
... is from overwork.

(I mean when is the last time you can remember
Death trying to take a day off.
It's just hard to picture Death relaxing in a hammock
or fiddling about in his basement woodshop.)

Anyway, he looked sort of lost, fidgeting through his paperwork.
He asked, "Is this 237 Oakdale Lane?"
"Yes," I replied.

"Are you sure, because I'm here to haul away the soul
of some work-obsessed maniac
who had a heart attack
while raking leaves on his day off.
Now, obviously this can't be you.
There is nothing in my notes about some silly flake
lying on a leaf strewn lawn muttering to his gardening tools."

Well, I knew that I couldn't fool a seasoned pro like Death for long.
I knew if I wanted to live,
I'd have to do something very convincing,
to prove that I wasn't the guy he was looking for.

So..? What would you do?

I looked up to where my neighbors had their leaves
packed in pristine plastic bags, and lined up neatly on the corner...

And I ran up to that corner...

and I pulled back my rake...

and I gave it a mighty swing!

And that first bag ripped open...

... the leaves danced in the wind!

I marveled at the sight... briefly.

...and ...I knew I was right...
that if I wanted to live...
I had better keep going...

So, I ran down the length of my street,
ripping row after row after row of leaf-packed plastic bags,
until naturally...
The cops were called!

Now, at my sanity hearing...

I told the tale you are hearing now.
Only I recounted the famous fable about the grasshopper,
that took up residence with a responsible ant
during the length of one long winter.

But there is a little known epilogue to that story,
I informed the court.

It seems that during the length of that winter,
the grasshopper taught the ant to play the fiddle.
Come spring, the ant quit his day-job,
and they have been traveling the countryside
as troubadours ever since.

And it's the same with me.

Once I truly heard music,

I could never go back
to a commuter line of drab ants ever again.

I offer this story,

as the only proof of my sanity.

I swear I'm not crazy.

By Chris Chandler and Philip Rockstroh
Originally published in *Protection from All this Safety* (1996)
and album *Hell Toupe* (1999)

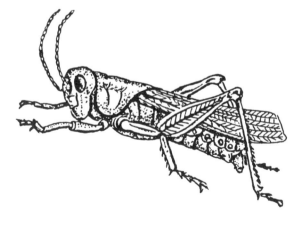

"I Am Not Making This Up!"

This is Not a Folk Song

Most of my stories start out with the phrase, "my car broke down."

Only, the time I'm thinking of,
the car didn't exactly break down. The engine fell out of the vehicle.

I don't know if you've ever had the engine fall out of your vehicle,
but trust me it is a sight to behold.
I wasn't sure what I was gonna do,
so I called up my oldest friend in the world,
and he said he'd be glad to drive
the three hours down from Atlanta to get to La Grange.
I sat on a milk crate and panhandled change.

I don't know, if you've ever tried to panhandle change
when you're wearing a t shirt that says
"Just Say No To a Real Job."

The folks of La Grange all seemed annoyed,
as I purchased a *Schlitz Malt Liquor* tall-boy,
and went back to my milk crate,
where I had to wait.

I shared my last cigarette,
with another vagrant,
who was peddling flowers.
We swapped stories and wasted the hours.

His story had it that – these two guys
got really drunk on Night Train or MD 20/20.
They were riding on a boxcar and got caught,
were thrown from the moving vehicle and subsequently killed.
His story has it that their bodies were so polluted
with Night Train and MD 20/20,
that since they were buried in a shallow grave
outside of Green Bay Wisconsin,

nothing will grow there to this day.
I had to tell my friend that I did not believe his story,
but I thought it was somehow,
beautiful.

But this is not a folk song,
It is about the way I feel.
And whether that's universal,
Who am I to tell, it's not a folk song,
But you are welcome to sing along.
But it ain't got no harmony and I think that that's OK.
Because, I'm not feelin' harmonious anyway.

This story is about my friend Frank.
Frank is my oldest friend in the world.
Our buildings faced each other down in Stone Mountain, GA
and we had rock wars against each other.
We went to kindergarten together.
We went through puberty together.
We went through juvenile delinquency together.
We even detoxed together.

When Frank got there he did what he always does.
He didn't say a word, he just handed me a bottle of tequila,
and we took off – past those shotgun distilleries.

I started laying it on thick and heavy to my friend Frank
about how I didn't think the last five years of my life
amounted to a damn thing – traveling around the country,
living in the back of a pickup truck,
maybe staying in homeless shelters
– writing songs about the people that I meet.

As I was getting deep into my self-pity rap,
I looked over to Frank for some sort of a response,
and he still hadn't said anything.
Instead, he just looked up,
which made me look up.

I noticed for the first time these giant iron butterflies
ejecting and rejecting their landing gear
– which could only mean one thing –
that we were headed towards the Atlanta airport
– the world's largest airport.

Frank exited at the last remaining exit in Hapeville, GA,
and we were on this little dirt road.
We were fishtailing along it, until we came up to a chainlink fence.
Frank, he nudged that chainlink fence with the front bumper of his car
and that gate swung open.
We were no longer near the Atlanta airport,
but we were in it!

And I don't mean in the parking lot!
I mean, me and my oldest friend in the world
had managed to get down between the runways...
and we were in fact...
dragracing a 727!

I thought for a minute we were going to win,
'cause we were about flying!

That is until we saw this other chainlink fence coming up on us real fast.
So Frank, he locked them down and we doughnuted around.
Frank hopped out of the car, pulled out a little white piece of paper,
and undid the combination lock, and pulled the pickup truck inside.

We were in about a twenty yard fenced-off area
that sits between the runways of the Atlanta airport.

But this is not a folk song,
It is about the way I feel.
And whether that's universal,
Who am I to tell, it's not a folk song,
But you are welcome to sing along.
But it ain't got no harmony and I think that that's OK.
Because, I'm not feelin' harmonious anyway.

Now the reason that twenty yard fenced-off area
sits there between the runways is
because... because... it is a graveyard.

Now in the state of Georgia you have to ask a family's permission
to move a graveyard, and my friend Frank's family
did not give the Atlanta Airport permission to move that tiny plot.

I looked down at some of the dates,
and they were all there from before the Civil War.
Now to find anything in the city of Atlanta from before
Sherman built the first interstate through to Charleston,
is relatively significant.

The date that caught my eye read,
"Emmanuel, age seven, House servant."

I went to ask Frank about that.
But Frank, he still hadn't said anything.

Instead, he had climbed up on top of the tallest monument.
So I climbed up there with him.
Drinking Tequila with my oldest friend in the world.
Watching the planes take off so close
that we could actually make out figures in the window.

I noticed from that height that the planes have to
jog left and then dart right to avoid this tiny graveyard.
I started thinking about my measly five years of living on the road
and how that might not ever amount to a damn thing.

But here was the life of one seven year old slave
who could change, or at least slow down,
the steamrollers of progress,
one hundred and fifty years after his death.

That, my friends, I thought,
was beautiful.

Written in Atlanta in 1993
Originally released on *Generica* (1994)

The Pageant of
the Paterson Silk Strike

I believe in Solidarity.

I believe in the Easter Bunny,
I believe in the Tooth Fairy,
I believe in Santa Claus.

I believe that the power of good is greater than that of evil,
–but not by very much.

I believe in the Buddha,
Mohammed,
Vishnu,
Jesus Christ,
I believe in Peanut Butter.

I believe that Athena sprang from the head of Zeus,
and that Atlas really held the world on his shoulders
(though I'm not sure where his feet were at the time.)

I believe it is the telling of the tale that makes it so.

I believe that children have imaginary friends,
and that adults really can't see them.
I believe that blankets have magical powers
that protects us from monsters.
(Perhaps that's why I believe in condoms.)

I believe that four-leafed clovers bring good luck.
I believe that people really do get abducted by aliens,
and that people who don't believe that,
never had an imaginary friend.

In 2001, I saw the image of the Virgin Mary
emerge from a rust stain on a metal telephone pole.

I pointed it out to others.
A crowd gathered.
People began to genuflect.

I believe that every picture tells a thousand stories
and every story paints a thousand pictures.
(You do the math.)

I believe that photographs, themselves, can speak.

In 2005 in Paterson, NJ, I saw a photograph taken in 1913,
of ten-thousand people gathered at a balcony,
listening to speakers shout their speeches with no sound system.

In the far corner of that photograph,
there is a small child, eight years old – born in 1905.
That child told me his story.

He said, "What's a hundred years between friends?"

In 1900, there were not 1900 automobiles,
or 1900 miles of paved roads to drive them on.

In 2000, there were enough miles of paved roads
to build a bridge from here to Uranus,
and enough assholes on the road to form a traffic jam.

In 1900, it cost two cents to get a letter
from Paterson, NJ to New York City
and it took two days to get it there.
In 2000, it cost thirty-eight cents,
and it took two days to get it there.

But what's a hundred years between friends?

In 1913, European imperial powers,
were about to begin slaughtering themselves wholesale
with mechanized warfare.

It had only been ten years since the Wright Brothers,
and already they were dropping bombs from planes.

In 1913, The Panama Canal opened, as did Grand Central Station.

Cracker-Jack introduced prizes for the first time.

Buffalo Bill Cody's Wild West show
could no longer compete with the new motion picture industry,
and went bankrupt.
The Wild West was over.

Richard Nixon was born.

The streets of America were frenzied with the sound of factories.

Women could not vote.

The Russian Revolution had not yet happened,
but its electricity could be felt on the streets
of Moscow, Berlin, Madrid, Seattle
and Paterson, New Jersey.

The sound of revolution is exactly as loud
as the sound of a rumbling stomach.

Some claimed automation would lead to a reduction in work oad
– just like some claim the home computer will reduce ours.

When the machine gun was invented,
people said,
"With this weapon there is no way we would have another war
with a weapon that could kill hundreds in seconds."
Yet, the imperial powers of Europe,
convinced the poverty-stricken
to throw their bodies into the wake of mechanized destruction.

The boy in the photograph
told me that he had lived to see his brothers do just that.

In 1913, Henry Ford developed the assembly line for automobiles.

That same year in Seattle – mechanized saw mills
had been turning the great forests of the west into toothpicks.
Sure, the first mudslides occurred,
but dental hygiene was at an all time high.
(Well, that is until The Industrial Workers of the World
led the great Saw Mill Strike of 1913.)

In Akron, OH, rubber workers were on strike.
In British Columbia, railroad workers.
A year earlier, the IWW had won
the *Bread and Roses* Strike of Lawrence, MA.

In Paterson, NJ, factory owners realized
that anyone who could convince someone else
to run in front of a machine-gun nest deserved a ribbon,
and the factories of Paterson ran eighteen hours a day
cranking out silk and fabric for ribbons.

The war to end all wars was just beginning,
and there was no shortage of officers needing ribbons.
Demand was as high as the profits,
but the workers were stretched beyond their limit.
So the owners introduced a four-loom system,
that they claimed would lessen the workload
– but in fact doubled it.

That was the cigarette that broke the camel's back.

Thousands went on strike.
Thousands were arrested,
including the boy in the photograph.
There is no jail cell strong enough
to withstand the rumble of a man's stomach.

The jail cells were the epicenter of an earthquake
felt all the way to New York City.
Those tremors caught the attention of the IWW

who put together one of the most organized strikes in history.

Rallies were held, weekly meetings.
Well-to-do families in NYC offered childcare.
The boy in the photograph lived for three months
in the home of Mabel Dodge, a prominent NYC heiress.
Celebrity speakers were brought in.
New demands were raised:
The eight-hour day, healthcare, women's suffrage.

Twenty-thousand people gathered at once
to raise their voices into the air.

But for every foot they moved forwards,
they were pushed back eleven inches.

The power of good is greater than that of evil
– just not by very much.

Picketers were killed. More were arrested.
But no matter how many workers were killed,
it was the mills that remained dead.
No amount of violence could make them come back to life.

The only thing that could break that picket line
is the mightiest force on earth
– the sound of a rumbling stomach.

Although they had never been hungry a day in their life,
It was the Greenwich Village Intellectuals who realized this first.
The earthquake erupting in Paterson, NJ
was just a tremor warning of the
Ten Days That Shook The World.

Later, Jack Reed's famous book would do just that.
But for now, he – a Greenwich Village intellectual –
began to work on a play.

After all, it is the telling of the tale that makes it so.

Why else would great stories only happen to great storytellers?

He took his new play and it turned it into a fundraiser,
(though you won't find his name in the program.)

Big Bill Heywood and Elizabeth Gurley Flynn spoke,
(though you won't see their names on the marquee.)

Famed scenic designer John Sloan created the set,
(though you will not find his name in the credits.)

No, instead you will find:

*"The Pageant of the Paterson Silk Strike
Performed by the Workers Themselves."*

Madison Square Garden was filled to capacity.
Critics sat in the aisles prepared to hate
this new propagandist art form.

The striking workers waited in the wings
– for in this play – the workers themselves would act out the events.
Yes, in June of 1913 one-thousand striking mill workers
joined Actors Equity in New York City to perform
one play, for one night.

They would tell their own tale.

When the curtain went up,
a whistle sounded as if to begin a new work day.
On stage it was 6 AM on a February morning.
The mills were alive, and it was the workers who were dead.
But soon, the workers began to think.
Soon they were singing together.
They sang *"La Marseillaise."*
The audience joined in the chorus.

Fear a movement that sings.

The Great Silk Strike had begun.
They were singing.
Together.

With each triumph the audience cheered.
With each setback, they booed.

No rock concert could recreate the enthusiasm of that crowd.
They made *Woodstock* seem like an episode of *American Idol*.
The boy in the photograph was there.
He was one of the tens of thousands in the audience at the end,
in standing ovation, fist in the air,
singing at the top of his tiny lungs:
The Internationale

"Arise ye prisoners of starvation.
Arise ye wretched of the earth.
For justice thunders condemnation,
A better world's in birth!
No more tradition's chains shall bind us.
Arise, ye slaves, no more in thrall;
The earth shall rise on new foundations,
We have been naught we shall be all.

'Tis the final conflict,
Let each stand in their place,
The International Union
Shall free the human race."

The play received overwhelming critical acclaim.
To this day it is considered one of the
most important moments in modern art.
I heard about it in art school,
before taking any interest in labor history.
Few performances could ever match
what happened on that stage, that night.
But as with too many great works of art – it lost money.

How could it not?

Too many people were let in for free.
How could they not?

How can you ask a family to pay to see a play their striking father is in?

You can't.
The boy in the photograph did not pay.
How could he?

Without further financial support the general strike began to decay.
The workers slowly went back to work.
Many would say it was a defeat and
even the end of the IWW itself.

But the truth is – it was only the beginning
– at least for their goals.

There is no way to undo the jubilation of that crowd,
just as there could be no such thing as victory
without first there being an understanding of defeat.

Listen to the Blues.

If dreams were real, there would be no need for dreams .
In a world of no dreams, we could only dream of dreaming.
The workers may not have gotten everything they asked for
– they asked for a lot.
We still do not have everything they asked for.
(We still deserve it and we were still right in asking for it.)

The truth is, they went back to work under prestrike conditions.
Their original grievance – the fourloom system
was not implemented for another decade.

But a few short years later, on March 14, 1917
Congress enacted what the *Pageant of the Paterson Strike* demanded:
the eight hour day.

Three years later women could vote!

There has always been a very fragile bridge built
between intellectuals and laborers.

Intellectuals intellectualize millworkers,
and weavers weave the clothes of the intellectuals.
They cannot be the same thing.

The bridge is there.
It is fragile.
It takes skill to cross it.
Few will make it.

It is why we tell tales about those who do.

Perhaps a play can make it across the bridge.
Perhaps a song.
Perhaps the photograph of
an eight year old boy hanging in a museum in Paterson, NJ
can cross that bridge.

Perhaps one-thousand striking workers
telling their own tale can cross that bridge.

Once crossed,
there is no end to what can be accomplished!

It is the telling of the tale that makes it so.

Just like the Easter Bunny,

and the Tooth Fairy,

and the greatest story ever told.

Written in Pittsburgh in 2004
Originally released on *American Storyteller Vol II* (2006)

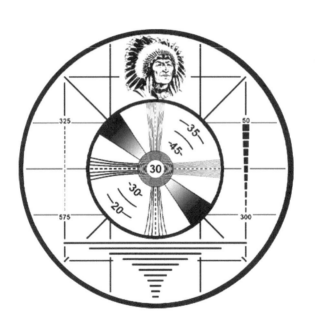

Prelude to Wounded Knee

In the United States of America in 2006, at a major tourist destination,
a 1994 Ford Escort pulls up and is surrounded
by young brown-skinned children begging for money for food.

This is not Calcutta or Bangladesh.
This is one of the most famous places,
a name on the tip of our tongues since we were in grade school.
We are talking about a major national monument,
in one of the richest countries in the world.

A little east of it, there are Egyptian-sized carvings of two great Americans:
Abraham Lincoln and Crazy Horse:
Contemporaries.

Two men – great leaders of great nations, that bordered each other.
They warred against one another, for the entirety of both of their lives.
Both men waged brutal war, for the good of their people,
and to preserve a way of life – yet they never met.

This is why I think to March of 1863,
when all was not well in this country.
The United States was losing a different war.

It was then that a delegation of sixteen American Indians were called upon
by Abraham Lincoln. It was feared the Confederates were making allegiances
with the Southern Plains Indians.

Indians, led by Yellow Wolf of the Kiowa, and Lean Bear of the Cheyenne,
as well as delegates from the Comanche, Arapahoe and Caddo,
came to Washington.

It was believed that an elaborate show of pomp and circumstance
would ally the Indians with the Union.
They were taken on grand tours of Washington, DC,
where they met with the President and, of course,

shown the huge arsenal that was – and still is – the United States.
Yellow Wolf suddenly fell ill of pneumonia and died.
He was buried with full military honors as a Head of State.

(America has always been good at such symbolic gestures.
Forty Acres and a Mule, *Remember the Maine*, *Martin Luther King Day*,
Mission Accomplished.)

His tribesman insisted that he be buried with the *Medal of Peace*
that was presented to his tribe by Thomas Jefferson via Lewis and Clark.
(They had helped the first white men only a few decades before,
and had brought the medal with him on his journey,
because they were told it would award them safe passage.)

His death received great attention in the press.
In the papers, it was reported that on his deathbed,
Yellow Wolf's last words were
"to tell his people to live at peace with the Pale Face."
No Indian heard him utter these words.

The delegation however, returned to their native lands,
having pledged their allegiance to the Union, not the Confederacy.
They believed that in doing so, they had achieved peace, and that massacres
like the one in Minnesota a year earlier would no longer happen.

When Lean Bear left the East, he was sporting an authentic chain-maille outfit
from the thirteenth century, obtained from PT Barnum in exchange for
allowing himself to be a curiosity in the *Greatest Show on Earth*.

He boasted that the white man was at war with himself.
That they would soon kill one another, and that
the Indian would be able to take his country back by next spring.

However, before the delegation had even arrived,
the United States had passed the *Homestead Act*,
giving away native lands to anyone who would settle it.

The Iron Horse whinnied, as it neared the station in Kansas City.
Great bursts of steam and blackened coal erupted from its fiery nostrils

as its gallop was reduced to a trot.

Lean Bear had noticed the Ohio countryside was bare,
and Buffalo herds were thinner than he had ever seen.
He feared for his people still many horizons away.

As the Iron Horse paused for watering, he was shocked to witness hundreds of
buffalo heads mounted on plaques, for sale at the station,
which operated its own taxidermy shop.

The planners of the trip had been careful to avoid such sights
en route to Washington, but seemed to forget on the way back.

(It seems the Native Americans too, had manifest destiny –
which when translated into Kiowa and back,
means "The future is obvious.")

Once back with the Cheyenne in Colorado,
he found anti-Indian sentiment amongst the Whites, at an all time high.

The government supplies they had been promised,
for remaining on a reservation, were not delivered.

Hungry and in search of food, Lean Bear and about two hundred Cheyenne,
were looking for buffalo, when they were stopped by fifty Colorado Troopers,
armed with new weapons made possible by the Civil War.

Reportedly, two hundred head of cattle had been stolen by someone,
somewhere, and these hungry Indians must be to blame.

As Lean Bear and his son rode ahead to approach the troopers, he waved his
papers in the air - papers pledging peace, and signed by Abraham Lincoln.

They were shot off their horses, and then shot again.

When his body was examined, he was holding the medal awarded him by,
and bearing the likeness of, Abraham Lincoln.
The rest of the two hundred in his party escaped, but only for a few days.
They were tracked by some seven hundred volunteers,

and massacred in the middle of the night.

The Massacre at *Sand Creek* was ordered by Abraham Lincoln,
with whom they had just met.
Among the dead, were many members from the sixteen member delegation.
Within a decade all would be killed.

At the battle of *Adobe Walls* in 1874, a Kiowa Indian was killed
wearing an authentic chain-maille uniform from the thirteenth century.

With the Southern Plains Indians defeated, the army could concentrate on the
Northern Plains.

The Southern Plains Indians were forced to immigrate to St. Augustine, Florida,
where they would serve out the remainder of their days, locked in the oldest
European settlement in North America – the Spanish fort at St. Augustine.
(But that is a different story.)

As for the Northern Plains Indians, their fate was not much different.

The 1994 Ford Escort pulls away from the national monument in South Da-
kota.

As we head for the Interstate, we notice the sign directing traffic
towards the site, has been neatly altered to change the words from
National Monument: The Battle of Wounded Knee,
to *National Monument: The Massacre of Wounded Knee.*
(But that too is a different story.)

We hit the entrance ramp to a highway, built less than a lifetime since
the last free Indians were mowed down with machine guns,
by the United States Army.

We crossed the country to Lewisburg, Pennsylvania,
to see the Federal Prison where Leonard Peltier is still imprisoned.

But that too, is a different story.

Written on the road in 2006
Originally Released on *American Storyteller Vol. I* (2006)

The Stone Mountain of Georgia

In the year of my birth,
Rev. Dr. Martin Luther King Jr, said in his *I Had a Dream* speech,
"Let freedom ring from the Stone Mountain of Georgia."
Because he longed for change to come to America.

The reason Martin Luther King mentioned my hometown,
was because at the time it was the home of a very powerful Ku Klux Klan
wreaking terror throughout the south land in which I was born.
Because of the Klan, it is also the home of the world's largest carving
– the *Confederate Memorial* where the stone images of
the three Confederate leaders are indelibly-chiseled on the side
of the mammoth slab of granite that inexplicably protrudes
from the Georgia red clay, larger than Mount Rushmore itself.

It was on this site, the modern Klan was formed,
in a ceremony that involved burning a cross from the mountain's summit.
The inferno was so large
it could be seen from the city of Atlanta some twenty miles away.
The inferno it represented was much larger.
The rebel revelers longed for no change to come to America.

It was in that setting that I came into this world.
I saw my town of three thousand grow on rally days
to ten thousand as hooded heroes marched through the town,
and as young girls threw flowers at their feet.

How could I not long to be among them?

I did.

Yes, I grew up a racist. How could I not?

You could blame me. I was a kid.
You could blame my parents, but how could they know any better?
Growing up in rural Alabama during the depression,
it did not seem like a place that change was going to come to.

You could blame my grandparents.

My grandmother was sixty at Brown Vs. Board of Education.
She did not know there needed to be change in America.

Upon the outcome of Brown Vs Board of Education,
the state of Georgia answered by changing her state flag.
It added the Confederate battle flag as if to say,
"Change was never going to come to Georgia."

I am probably the youngest person you will likely meet
that went to a segregated school.
In 1970, Jimmy Carter succeeded Lester Maddox as governor
and went about practically desegregating the last of the segregated schools.

Change was coming to Georgia.

I was in the first grade.

I played football on the first desegregated little league team in my county:
The Central DeKalb 85 lb Packers.
Before they were The Packers they were known
as… yes… The Crackers.

Donning a 'University of Georgia G' on our helmets,
I found myself on the opposite end of the America I had known.
The University of Georgia did not
desegregate its football team for several years.
But with The Packers, I learned to depend on, play with,
sacrifice for my black teammates.

Team work.

When The Packers played teams in counties more isolated than De Kalb,
I found my team, and therefore myself,
on the receiving end of jeers and threats,
and even getting into sand lot brew-ha-has defending…
defending.. well, my team, but vicariously, desegregation.

Change is afoot,
(lets give it a hand.)

The white flight that inevitably parallels a growing city
blew right past Stone Mountain,
leaving in its wake a suburban black middle=class.

Soon the words *Stone Mountain* were on the front page
of *The New York Times,* for a second time in her history,
when the town that Martin Luther King
had singled out, elected a black mayor.

Change was brewing in America.
Today, only some old-timer whites remain.
My mother is one of them.

I came to visit her recently.
At the corner of Rockbridge Road and Cynthia McKinney Blvd
(named for another African-American that ran for president this year),
there is a Shell station which is down the street from my mother's house
and the Tupac Shakur Peace Park.

There, a young African-American middle-class teenager approached me
wearing his mall bought Negro League baseball jersey,
(made in Bangladesh)
and his gangsta-wannabe blood-diamond bling saying,
"You have no idea where you is."

I do.

One visible sign that change is at hand, is that in 2008,
a black teenager was willing to take a ride
with a middle-aged, oddly-clad, bald white man.

I took him to the old city hall, now a museum.
I showed him The Bell,
presented to the town by the King Foundation
to "Let Freedom Ring."

I took a drink from the colored water fountain,
I was not allowed to drink from as a child.
He in turn drank from the "white."

Parts of my childhood I am glad to have
relegated to the annals of small town museums.
In this last election, the city of Stone Mountain
carried Barack Obama ,
but not the state of Georgia.

But more importantly he carried the nation,
and…
the vote of my mother.

Change has come to America.

Let freedom ring from the Stone Mountain of Georgia.

Congratulations Barack Obama,

But more importantly,

Congratulations,

America.

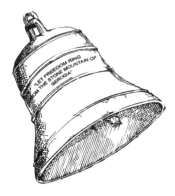

Written in Washington, DC in January 2008
Originally released on *So, Where Ya Headed?* (2009)

Wyoming

I was driving through Wyoming,
when my GPS stopped working.
It… made me mad.

"WHAT? No coverage!" I thought.

I remembered my first trip through
rural Wyoming twenty-five years ago.
I was just starting to book gigs,
and I HAD to make a phone call to New York City.

I had just booked a gig there,
and believe me, coming from Stone Mountain Georgia,
that was a big deal.

Only the signs on the highway read
"NO FOOD, NO SERVICES, NO PHONE,"
and they meant it.

When I finally found a phone, it was literally
a single phone booth in the middle of nowhere,
surrounded by giant rocks and a sky as big as Canada.

There were a couple of cars parked
and a line of people waiting to use the phone.
There was a bench to wait on.

Just twenty years ago, big swaths of this country
did not even have payphones.
These days you can't find a payphone either,
but it is for very different reasons.

Oh, how we love to reminisce the 'good old days'.
The ones that never were.

The days that we tattoo on our psyches,
or maybe even our bodies
to remember a particular moment in time.

I remember as a kid,
there was a guy in my elementary school with a tattoo.
I was afraid of him. I wanted to be like him.
It was the first tattoo I had ever seen close up.
It was a skull with a jester's cap.
I am not from this new generation of suburban white rebels
that have opened up tattoo parlors in shopping malls.

The Skull with the Jester's Cap?
The Grateful Dead were not exactly a part of my childhood.
The Jerry Garcia Transformer Robot Doll
had not yet been marketed.

The image disturbed me for years, but then I thought,
"What do you want your legacy to be?
A skull with a Jester's Cap?
Living your life making people laugh!
And when you die – you're still doing it."

The image of the tattoo grew in my head.
It became elaborate, decorated, bejeweled, magnificent.
To this day, whenever I see a tattoo
it always pales in comparison to my memory
of the one I had seen as a child.

Recently, I was in my hometown,
when I ran into the kid with the tattoo.
I got the chance to tell him how much the image had meant to me.
That I had spent the past twenty years of my life
traveling across the country, trying to make people laugh,
and I hope that after I die, I will still be doing it.

I managed to talk him into taking his shirt off so I could see it.
And there it was, in all its...   ...reality.

It looked like a prison tattoo.
Thin pale blue lines sagging from aging flesh.
He said he had done it himself, with a sewing needle and a ballpoint pen,
and was considering getting it removed.

I thought, "laughter dies, not from age, but from vanity"
(and in this case...laser surgery.)

Now, the reason I had been in my hometown
was to visit my mother, who was aging.
My siblings had called me to say it was time to come visit – and I did.

Only once I got there, I managed to catch a stomach virus.
I found myself in bed – my childhood bed.

I looked up, and there she was,
struggling down the hall with her walker,
oxygen tubes trailing behind her,
carrying a bowl of chicken noodle soup.

She put a thermometer in my mouth.
It was the same one she had
placed in my mouth as a child.
"A hundred and three degrees."
She wiped my forehead with a cool washcloth.

Oh, how the tables turn!
I had come home to help take care of her,
but she found strength from my illness.
It was the only time in my life
I can remember, I was glad to be sick.

The only thing I could do was to lay back
and savor the taste of chicken noodle soup, and saltines.

I knew It would be the last time,
my mother,
would ever mother me.

Written in Stone Mtn, GA 2008
Originally released on the album *So, Where ya Headed?* (2009)

THINK OUTSIDE THE BOX.

THE END

Discography

1988   *Neo Folk Guitar* (Cassette)
1989   *Stranded Musician Needs Gas out of Town* (Cassette)
        What, For This Price You Want Packaging too? (Cassette)
1990   *In The Road* (Cassette)
1991   *A Funny Thing Happened on The Way to The Abyss* (Cassette)
1992   *As Seen on No TV* (CD, Cassette)
1993   *Goin' Down The Road Feelin' Bad* (Book)
1994   *Stark Raving Chandler* – with Amanda Stark (Cassette)
        Generica – with Amanda Stark (CD)
1995   *Chandler Speaks and Won't Shut Up* (Cassette)
1996   *Protection From All This Safety* – with Philip Rockstroh (Book)
        If I Had Any Hits These Would Be The Greatest (Cassette)
1997   *Convenience Store Troubadours* – with David Rovics, Samantha Parton
        and Oliver Steck (CD)
1998   *Collaborations* – with Peter Yarrow, Dan Bern, Ellis Paul, Dar Williams,
        Martin Sexton, Jim Infantino, The Austin Lounge Lizards, Catie
        Curtis, Trout Fishing In America, Mike West and Tom Prasada-Rao. (CD)
1999   *Hell Toupee* – with Frankie Hernandez, Laura Freeman and Chad
        Austinson (CD)
2000   *Posthumously Live* – with Magda Hiller (CD)
2002   *Flying Poetry Circus* – with Anne Feeney (CD)
2003   *Fifteen Years on the Road and I'm Gonna Make it Home Tonight*
        (CD Anthology)
2004   *Live From the Wholly Stolen Empire* – with Anne Feeney (CD)
2005   *American Storyteller Vol I* (CD)
2006   *American Storyteller Vol II* (CD)
2007   *American Storyteller Vols III & IV* (CD Set)
2008   *Fifty from Twenty* (Anthology Boxed Set 4 CDs 1 DVD)
2009   *So, Where Ya Headed?* – with Paul Benoit (CD)
2010   *THE MUSE AND WHIRLED RETORT* - Anthology (Book)
2012   *Matadors* – with Paul Benoit (CD)
2013   *Avoiding Godot, Anthology* (Book)